I0115936

Know Yourself Melancholic

by Alexander Carberry

COPYRIGHT
KNOW YOURSELF MELANCHOLIC

© Alexander Carberry 2023

First Edition published by:

Bahr Press

Cross Street Business Centre

43a Cross Street, Suite 10

Burton-upon-Trent, Staffordshire, DE14 3AR

United Kingdom

All rights reserved. No part of this publication may be reproduced, stored in any retrieval system or transmitted in any form or by any means, electronic, mechanical, photocopying, recording or otherwise without the prior permission of the publishers.

Written by: Alexander Carberry

Editor: Uthman Ibrahim-Morisson

Cover photograph: © CANVA

Cover Design: Alexander & Baraka Carberry

A catalogue record of this book is available from the British Library.

ISBN-13: 978-0-9564513-4-7

About The Author

Alex Carberry was born in London, England. He was raised in Guyana, South America, on the edge of the Amazon. He returned to the United Kingdom to study, but after meeting with a Sufi teache~r, he chose instead to embark upon the Sufic path. He has spent 30 years studying Sufism, philosophy, geo-politics and Daoist martial arts. He is a practising herbalist and resides in Burton-upon-Trent, England.

Contents

Dedication

It is not that human beings are somehow inherently evil, but that we often do not doggedly support the good we see in them. It is, perhaps, that we do not excuse their shortcomings as committedly as we excuse our own. And moreso, that often we do not trust in ourselves.

This book is dedicated to becoming better at doing these things.

—Alex Carberry Ramadhan 2023

Introduction

Welcome! Well, you have read Know Yourself: Discover Your True Nature with the Ancient Sufic Wisdom. You've had a long think about it, you've overcome a lot of doubt, and finally come to the conclusion that you are a Melancholic. But as a Melancholic you still may not be sure, or sure enough with a healthy dose of doubt, or unsure with just enough doubt to be sure enough to doubt it. This is a book about Melancholics, and for those who wish more insight into this incredibly thoughtful personality type. By this book we expect you to have gained some clarity as to what your personality type is, or at least, that of those around you. You take a lot longer than other types to work these things out, and that is ok. It is just the way that you're wired. Being able to accurately predict the behaviour of others is certainly fun and useful. Apple trees produce apples, and they do not produce pears, unless you've grafted a pear tree onto an apple tree (Yes, you Melancholics, we know how your minds work!). People are just what they are, as that hidden music to which we are all dancing blows through us, driving us along the journey of life; all different notes, scales and scores in the symphony of human variety.

If you are reading this book out of interest, and you are not a melancholic, expect it to be fascinating. You will grasp the nature of the Melancholic with greater clarity and will see the vast variety found within this type. Trees may be trees but look at the endless variety of trees, and even at the notable differences within a single species. Apple trees may be apple trees, but there is such variety! Often, people complain that the idea of being a particular type is so limiting, deterministic and simplistic. I smile because if we did not possess some measure of a fixed form, self-development would be impossible, for it is the great uniformity in our responses that allows us to see over time, that our responses have patterns. This allows us to reflect and to realise that we can make changes to our patterns of responses. I don't smile over the doubters, but over the impossibility of working at self-development without something of a predictable form. Your type reveals your energetic signature, and we shall see that no two Melancholics are the same, despite the striking similarities that characterise Melancholics. Melancholics must think, consider many options and possibilities, and invariably must think of all of the things that could go wrong, because if they can then there is a chance that they will and so they should think of all the possibilities well in advance. A Melancholic is a Melancholic and that is just the way that they're wired.

A Melancholic is a Melancholic

As a Melancholic, you are in harmony with the Element Earth. The earth is very similar to you. It is fixed, firm and dependable. It supports movement, but from deep within, as with trees, which grow in it, and are sustained by it. The earth changes slowly, and you are the same. You bring thought as if from the depths of a deep cave within the earth and you are foundational, thinking things through and preparing for the worst. Your season is Autumn. During autumn the bright green leaves and incredible colour of the flowers begin to withdraw into the winter. Browns, siennas, burnt oranges, and very dark greens persist. Life is withdrawing into its depths for the long, cold stillness of winter. Activity is retreating, and the environment is preparing itself for the lengthy, cold bleakness of winter. It is a time for storing, in preparation for the difficult, cold months ahead. Your harmony brings a storing, preparing nature, and a natural calm. It is important to grasp this underlying harmony, for it reveals the secret of your purpose, and of your natural, inherent strengths and weaknesses. Melancholics love thought, reflection and preparation, and so will be found standing back from the crowd, but you play a vital role. We will be exploring the Melancholic, and their various combinations in detail, and you will find yourself within this, but you will, of course, have to do a lot of thinking to see if you agree or disagree with me. You will get a lot more than you bargained for. You will disagree often, and then think for months at a time sometimes, but I'm afraid that you'll discover that I was right. Now, though that is irritating, I'm afraid that it is right! I know that I am right! So, good luck. You're not the first Melancholic and you won't be the last. The challenges that you face as a Melancholic are as old as mankind, and as you get a handle on the way that you work, I promise you that it will be interesting, and you will understand why we have fun observing you. You are what you are and you play an incredibly important role in the human theatre.

So, we'll get on with the study of the biological occurrence that is the Melancholic. For you, much will be uncomfortable, but I can guarantee that once you get your head around it, you will find it liberating.

You're a Melancholic, and that's just the way you're wired!

Apple Trees Do Not Produce Bananas

Apple trees do not produce bananas, cherries, pears, grapes, mangoes, plums or anything else but apples. You are a melancholic, and you have a tendency to see the problems and defects in things. Often Melancholics don't like being Melancholics, but you are. Once you get over this, and start to see the great qualities that you possess, accepting that you will never be anything else, then you will surrender to unleashing the incredible capacity of your type. This fixed form that you have to work with, rather than limiting you, gives you incredible abilities with which to engage the world and grow. You will be free to mold, change and transform yourself through the fundamental pattern material which makes you up. As you express the energetic signature that is you, you will uncover countless ways to sing your

Melancholic song. You will always recognise the music of Thelonious Monk, Charlie ('Bird') Parker, Charles Mingus, John Coltrane or Miles Davis. The distinctiveness of their creative genius sings through their work. The sound of Sarah Vaughan, Solomon Burke, Sam Cooke, Minnie Ripperton, Janis Joplin, Roberta Flack or Gregory Porter, is always distinctive. We are all like that. There is a music singing through us. Our voices, gestures, the cadence of our footsteps, our DNA, all characterise us and sing our unique song. That is what those who love us love, and those who hate us hate. It helps us to realise the futility of trying to please everyone. We are here to sing our song clearly, for we can truly sing no one else's. You are you and there is not another one like you, and never again shall you occur. No one else can ever be you. We can develop, change, grow and refine ourselves, but throughout, we are working with that distinctive song that is us. That fundamental, energetic signature will always be expressed. Do you get it? You are you! This method is about you accepting yourself, being who you are and learning to express the best of your possibilities, whilst accepting that at times you will express your worst. So, we get up, sort ourselves out, reorientate and continue on our journeys.

Your song is the expression of the breath of life, which blows through you, blowing only as it will blow through you. This energetic signature is your psyche or soul. What we are learning to read is the very patterning of our souls. Apple trees do not produce bananas and that's just the way it is!

The Forest and the Trees

Your personality type is like a forest of oak trees. Oaks are a family, but each oak tree is different. Amongst Oak trees are trees which possess similar traits. Just look at the different types of Quercus, (for Quercus is the family of oaks). We will learn to recognise the different kinds of Melancholic with precision and an understanding of how they differ.

What You Will Get From This Book

You will of course learn about Melancholics and even more about Melancholics and the way they work. If you want to learn about the other types then read the other books:

- Know Yourself: Sanguine

- Know Yourself: Choleric

- and Know Yourself: Phlegmatic

These other books explore the other types but this book is exclusively about Melancholics. We will develop the ability to examine ourselves in the manner of an artist looking at a painting and seeing with attention to detail, the brushstrokes, the hues, tones and richness of the colour. As we listen to the song we will recognise the scales, the harmonies, the modes, the moods, the rhythms, the tempi, and all the richness and specificity of the performance. We are developing upon this journey the ability to see the texture, tones, hues, tempi, scales and brushstrokes of our selves, and to examine others with the same tools that you have used to examine yourself. Now, how's that for efficiency! As you develop this remarkable capacity to see and examine others, you can adjust and modulate your interactions to better harmonise with those around you. These skills will remain yours forever, and you will be able to use them to understand your greatest wealth! And what is your greatest wealth? It is nothing less than your own self!

By getting to know yourself you will learn to know others.

You will gain incredible tips on dealing with yourself and aspects of your personality that you may find difficult. I will give you tips on how to use those difficult aspects to your own advantage and you will also gain insights into your own genius. The word genius in its original Latin is, 'your natural inclination and natural abilities'. You will learn to accept and harness your natural genius. As you learn to discover, work with and play with your natural genius, you will also learn to avoid the areas in which you are inherently weak. Once you enter into an arena in which you are naturally weak, you will learn to employ the strategies of those that are naturally strong in these arenas, to your own best advantage. In these environments you will require a plan to keep you out of trouble. In life we have to face the risks of entering into spaces which are beyond our present capacities. Taking risks is an opportunity for personal growth.

For the non-Melancholics, I promise to give you lots of tips for dealing with Melancholics. Though Melancholics themselves will insist that you understand the reasons why they did what they did, and you almost went mad listening to their detailed explanations, please allow me to inform you that they may well have been right! Melancholics are all about understanding, and things making sense (even when they don't!). I intend to be generous. We will keep in the spirit of the series, and as you know, these books are short and packed with tips, so within the constraints of size I will give you loads more than most Melancholics think I should.

Let Others Be What They Are

We may often have ideals of human behaviour. The problem is that people are just people, and regardless of our wonderful ideals they will just be what they are. Human nature has ranges of possibilities and they will all be expressed. The Know Yourself method helps us to become more accepting of ourselves and others, in all of our good qualities and our faults. By helping us to understand our own underlying patterns, we soon grasp that others are subject to their own energetic ebb and flow. Human beings cannot be molded according to our whims and fancies, and when we do succeed, we discover that it has unintended consequences. We all have needs, impulses and energetic patterns, which constitute our fundamental natures, and which will always express themselves in a multitude of ways. It's just the way we're wired!

However, this does not excuse bad behaviour. We cannot make the excuse that, 'This is just the way I am!', after behaving badly, because injustice always unleashes its own dynamic, for there is a hidden balance in the universe and injustice will express its Karmic redress. The excuse will just make our eventual suffering worse. Making amends for our bad behaviour, brings justice into our social situation and dampens the Karmic redress. Seeking forgiveness often stops the dynamic and can bring love between people who previously experienced mutual enmity. It is in our interest to right our wrongs and improve our behaviour as we journey through the world. Not to do so is to release upon the world terrible social consequences, which can be prevented by the frequent and sincere use of, 'Sorry!', 'Please forgive me!', 'I didn't realise that this would have hurt you so deeply!', 'I'm sorry I don't know what overcame me but it won't happen again!', I think that you get the idea. Bad manners and bad behaviour remains what it is and, 'This is just the way that I'm wired!', does not excuse bad manners and inappropriate conduct.

Developing ourselves, improving our characters and becoming wiser in our responses, is a lifetime's work. Since we can only change ourselves, and others have to change themselves, the onus is upon you to do something about you, and for them to do something about them. Until they change just assume that what they do reveals the manner in which they are wired until they consistently change their actions. However, we will always see the revelation of the fundamental pattern of our nature in our everyday behaviour.

When faced with other people's bad behaviour, despite our efforts to improve ourselves, people often say, 'It is not fair!'. Well, it's not! So, get over it! You get to grow and they can choose to grow or to stunt their growth and you can choose to join them in stunting yours.

Who Should Read This Book

Read this book if you have read, 'Know Yourself: Discover Your True Nature With The Ancient Sufic Wisdom', which is the first book in the series, or if you have read another book on personality types which has helped you to understand which of the four types you are (Sanguine, Choleric, Melancholic or Phlegmatic). If you are reading this book then you should be a Melancholic or interested in finding out about Melancholics.

How To Read This Book

Go through the contents page, and take a quick look at anything that arouses your attention. This will stimulate your interest, provide you with an overview of the book's structure, as well as encourage you to read it. It may also be helpful to read the book from cover to cover once quickly. Things are much easier to remember and make use of if you remember their context. After reading through once, then return to the parts that you feel necessary to re-read and reflect upon.

Discuss some of the concepts with those around you. One of the easiest ways to learn and remember is to share what you know. Question those who have known you for a long time about the way they see you. Observe carefully the way you and others do things. Remember, you do not have to like something for it to be true. Some truths are horribly bitter to begin with, but precisely therein lies their sweetness, for things can only be what they are, and the energy spent trying to make things what they are not, is certainly energy wasted. You will discover much about yourself that you like and much that you do not like. What we are working towards is not liking what we see, but surrendering to the truth or reality of things as they are. The colour red does not change because we may dislike it! We may change the shade, tone and hue of red but redness always remains redness. Our fundamental nature is analogous to colouring in this respect. Read the book, make your observations and once they become truly clear to you, accept them. Remember, the stories that we tell ourselves about ourselves and everything else, are just stories; the way things really are transcends our stories. Over time our dislike and resistance to the way things are will change to acceptance and we will be free to work with what is there, rather than attempting to maintain an illusion. Over time and with practice our need to persist with our stories in the face of reality diminishes.

Welcome To The Journey

Congratulations! You have made it this far. Let us continue our journey into the depths of our personality type, to encounter the treasures, discoveries and wonders. I continue to be fascinated by this knowledge and am really excited about sharing it with you. I hope that you will be even more fascinated than I have been and I pray that you will continue to find it more and more useful, as you continue the work upon yourself.

The amazing thing about the Universe is that just the act of discovering something new and changing yourself, means that the entire Universe has in fact changed. Everything is changing and yet it all remains the same!

Transformation is the very nature of the Universe and you are not separate from it. You were born to be what you are and to be the best that you can be.

> Will the reward of doing good be anything
>
> Other than good?
>
> So which of the favours of your Lord do
>
> You both deny?
>
> **The Noble Qur'an: 55:60-61**

The Pure Melancholic

Introduction

He was well dressed. The shirt was neatly ironed and seamed. The dark trousers and jacket, revealed his quiet taste. He was always neatly dressed. From beneath his furrowed brow, his eyes shone intently, as he considered the activities in the room. He recognised his old friend Susan and walked over to greet her. They stood in the corner and continued a conversation that they had left off, the last time they met two months ago. He explained his points, methodically and paused to think often, as Susan nodded. She knew him well and allowed him to develop his arguments and she valued his intelligence. He stood apart and did not easily join the noise of the crowd. When their conversation ended he considered his next move, as he wound his way through the party.

But it was tiring and so after a few hours of this he began to think of going, the noisy chatter, the loud music and the girl that he would like to speak to but just couldn't find the right moment to start, something was always not just right and a stream of valid sensible excuses would stop him from going forward and would often make interactions a little awkward. It felt a little like a thick soup of obstacles that he just couldn't wade through. The cut patterns of the well balanced heavy crystal glass attracted his attention and so he sat down brooding and looking at the geometrical pattern and wondering how they made it. Lost in thought the noisy chatter, the loud music and the girl he wanted to speak to withdrew from the forefront of his attentions and he brooded quietly, in his corner. A strong desire to go home began to creep up upon him, then he felt the sensation of eyes boring into him intently and looked up, and there she was staring at him, and when he looked up, she looked away. Two Melancholics! This will be fun!

Description Of The Melancholic

The Melancholic is a creature of thought. This active inner life is often accompanied by a level of social coldness. It seems that the inner activity sacrifices some of the outer social intelligence. So that they are often withdrawn from people and will take a long time to get to know you. They spend a long time clarifying their thoughts, and working through their ideas rationally. They will even rationalise feeling.

When speaking you have to explain everything and others will be compelled to hear the whys and wherefores. You are not a particularly expressive type. With you the soundness of the argument is everything. When on the rare occasion you are very expressive then know that this is a thing about which you truly feel deeply and passionately. You generally take a while to build and deliver your point and you need space and active listening to support your delivery of that point.

You like to close your options down and tend to not be very flexible. Flexibility with you comes either by incredible practice or the influence of your servant type. You will generally box yourself in to get to action and to have a clear idea of your goal.

You may not generally be the most generous but you often do come prepared for all eventualities, and you have thought about the things that the other types have not.

Of course with all this thinking comes the Melancholic gift to the world: Procrastination!

The Melancholic in Action

Sara walks into the dinner party exquisitely dressed. She is unbelievably neat and everything matches. She steps through the crowd with a quiet reserve,, greeting as she goes, heading for an oasis of safety, where she can engage but have some space, or at least refuge with some familiar friends (familiar people will do). She sits down and remembers that a bit of the chalky Southern Spanish dust brushed onto the hem of her trouser suit, so when she sits down, it is deftly brushed off, but that might not have been enough. Platitudes were exchanged for about fifteen minutes, during which an irritating and tiresome man (a sanguine) kept invading her space, so Sara gets up and heads for the toilets, fixes her makeup and daubs, once and for all, the chalky dust from the hem of her trouser leg with a small, carefully dampened hand towel. She looks into the mirror checking her makeup and working out whether that irritating sanguine might have gone, whether she would return to the same spot, whether Natalie (an old friend) was still sitting outside on the terrace with her friends and she should join them, how would it be to join the dancing (but she wouldn't do so with that irritating man), how brave she had been to come alone, She fixes her lipstick and that work problem comes up again, but this time she has a solution, 'Eureka!' A slight smile flashes across her face like a swift, passing cloud. She decides upon Natalie and then takes the long way to the terrace past the bar to avoid that irritating sanguine. Joining Natalie she finds a comfortable spot on the edges of the group, whips out her phone and quickly outlines her work solution with a few key words to remember. Listening to the conversations and thinking about what is being said, she occasionally joins in. The irritating sanguine appears scanning the crowd and so she shrinks back into her chair awkwardly, trying to become invisible.'What is the matter with him?', 'I hope that he isn't looking for me!' 'Why does that self-centred git not leave me alone?' Natalie catches her eye and mouths silently, That is the guy I was telling you about.' She comes over and whispers into Sara's ear, 'He's my boss who keeps asking about you, saying that he rarely sees you around, he practically begged me to invite you, remember?'.Sara wishes that the earth would open up and swallow her! Not him! Well, he is charming but ... 'Good God, his colours are so bright!' She thinks. She takes too long to reply and so Natalie takes the initiative and calls him over, Sara could have killed her, and later on she probably will (slowly and painfully).

Man! Is there a lot going on below the surface with Melancholics? Don't be fooled by the quiet exterior. Like Swans' feet, their minds are paddling away furiously below the surface. What Sara doesn't realise yet is that Melancholics often marry Sanguines and they will discover why as they now begin an exchange that she can deem safe enough to open up.

This is a description of a very strong Melancholic in whom we can see very little evidence of the other elements or personality types. Some of this, if not all of it, will probably ring true for you.

The World According to the Melancholic

Let us imagine a Melancholic describing themselves. It is probably a CV or an interview:

I would describe myself as a thinker and problem solver. I love to work things out. Things need to be put into order and ordered even when there is apparent disorder all around me, I am just not comfortable when there isn't this sense of order. I tend to be methodical and deliberate and prefer a slower pace. I will home-in on a problem with a steady, deliberate approach and I need lots of personal space to work through things. I particularly hate it when people crowd me, especially when I am working things through, and will tend to lash out or sulk. I need space and you will not get the best out of me by crowding or rushing me unnecessarily.

I love repetitive tasks, keeping things organised and improving the efficiency of repetitive tasks. This doesn't necessarily mean that I do boring! I need a challenge but I can do repetitive, and by that I don't mean mechanical. Mechanical is for machines. If an eye for detail, thinking, organizing, problem solving and being a stickler for method is required, then I am definitely the person that you are looking for. I thrive under these conditions.

When I do something I want it to be perfect and it is for this reason that I tend to procrastinate. I want to commit when the conditions are perfect. There is always something else that I would like to have for the project. The upside of this is that I over-prepare for eventualities. When I go at a project we will have what we need, and more.

I am not a people person but I can do people. When I work with people I need personal space. You will find that I tend to think through what I am going to say before I have said it, so I am careful with words.

Things I Hate

Disorganisation! I hate disorganised situations. Rushing into things unprepared. I really don't get people who do that! Useless, endless chatter. Not thinking things through. I particularly hate it when a project has no clear goals and doesn't make sense. When we set out we should already know where we are going. I need to be clear about what I am doing, how I am getting there and what we have in order to get things done and arrive at the destination. Some people want flexibility but I need clarity, I hate fuzzy thinking and a lack of clear focus.

I love silence and find people who just chatter nervously into the silence difficult. Ok, I hate that!

I hate it when people interrupt me as I develop an idea. They want to get to the point quickly whilst I need to develop and make my point. My point will be rational and I hate irrational ideas.

I hate excessive optimism, and excessive positivity really irritates me. A good method, consistency and determined organisation are a much better indicator of success than all the optimistic, positivity nonsense. Things go wrong, and when they do we need to be ready, and I hate it when people don't want to examine what goes wrong, for invariably, things have more chance of going wrong than they do of going right. For these reasons Sanguines can really irritate me!

My Outlook

I think that life can be wonderful if we can organise ourselves and have the space and time to do wonderful things. So routines, discipline and thinking things through go a long way to producing a happy life. There is work and there is fun, day and night, good and bad. We need clarity, and to understand the nature of what we are involved in.

When you ask me a question I will think through the answer and the devil is in the detail so expect me to give you detail and my justifications for my answers. If that is not what you want, why waste time asking me questions. As you know, I have an eye for detail and will give you detail and logical arguments. My silences indicate that I am thinking things through and I would prefer you not to interrupt them. I live my life in a rational and sensible way.

The Melancholic According to the Rest of the World

It is really useful to see yourself through the eye of others. We learn to empathise with their view and to gain other perspectives on ourselves, beyond the story patterns that we would normally tell about ourselves. It can make all the difference, but it is invariably uncomfortable. When it makes you squirm then know that you are really onto something useful.

The Good Points

> Excellence is never an accident. It is always the result of high intention, sincere effort, and intelligent execution; it represents the wise choice of many alternatives - choice, not chance, determines your destiny.
> – **Aristotle**

When Aristotle said this he was probably thinking of a Melancholic and he himself was a Melancholic Choleric.

Melancholics have beautifully organised minds, natural discipline and are usually dependable. They are such sticklers for detail that there are some activities in which they are just the best and we love them for this. They are not necessarily fun, but they can be good, solid, dependable friends. And melancholic wit is wry, sometimes acerbic and clever. They are such perfectionists.

They are either tidy or untidy, but always organized, and their disciplined organisation is something that we often have to turn to (Often resentfully!). They bring such reason and rationality and will have a solid reason for everything. If that were not enough, you will have solutions and tools for the many eventualities that you think of. You are resourceful.

As a close friend you notice things and when balanced you are very considerate. You will not forget our birthdays, favourite colours, favourite foods, who our friends are, etc. You carry a compendium in your head!

The Complaints

Oh dear, where do I start? I really don't want you to sulk. Well, that is my first complaint, 'You sulk!'. Instead of talking things through and letting us understand, you sulk your way through and make our lives miserable, if we let you. You are a master or mistress of all that passive aggressive stuff. Getting through to you in order to understand the reason for your sulking is for the brave and selfless, and you take your pound of flesh as we struggle through the minefield (or minefields). We really won't automatically know what has upset, offended or riled you, without you making it clear, and yet you speak your feelings in riddles! In case you haven't noticed, you don't speak your feeling space well, and so getting these things out of you is akin to pulling the teeth out of a chicken.

Some types are thick skinned, but you definitely are not. You get upset easily and your penchant for 'history' means that you will often string together past perceived slights, actual slights and other things into a seamless private narrative.

You see problems first and orient yourself from the perspective of the problems. Then due to your incredible intellect and rationality you frame the situation rationally in these terms and sometimes breaking through this narrative in order that we gain a more balanced approach can be very difficult. When we other types resort to our other strengths (such as charisma, great story telling, inspirational persuasion and our other tools), you can become quite upset and feel not listened to. The Choleric's targeted dismantling of the Melancholic argument and position is a classic example of this, and it often brings bad blood. The problem actually being that you are so taken in by your own rationality that you often cannot empathise with other ways of seeing the same issue.

You can often lack flexibility and the more tired you are the worse it gets. Learning to empathise and see other approaches natural to the other types will help, and it will actually strengthen your Melancholic genius, but getting you there is hard work! By the time you do get there you tend to be a hell of a lot more flexible.

You delve deeply into things and when we ask you a question, instead of an answer you give us a guided underwater tour of the entire ocean!

When we are making a solution to cross a river you want to give us a solution that can cross a river, become a submarine in an ocean, survive twelve months without food underwater, be self repairing, be fuel efficient, survive ocean storms with waves of over one hundred feet and reach a cruising speed of one hundred kilometres per hour. When we tell you that the river is only three hundred metres wide and twenty five metres deep, you present us with 'what if' scenarios. We want a solution that takes fifteen minutes and you want something that takes two years to build. Oh, and then you procrastinate!

You procrastinate! Yes you do! If procrastination were a cash crop you would be a trillionaire!

You are incredibly loyal and principled. Though we love your loyalty, your principles often take you to places in which you lose sight of the people involved and become intoxicated by your ideals and principles. Since your loyalty and principles seem to emerge from the same impulse it really becomes problematic. We wish that your loyalty and principles could decouple and your principles could become wisdom which sees the entire situation not from the perspective of ideals but from the messy realities of people, their dramas and the interconnections of living. You become ensconced in the entire messy realities in the capsule of your principled ideals and it seldom ever helps. Then having secured the moral high ground you are then intolerable!

And you are stubborn, gloriously stubborn. So gloriously stubborn that it is legendary. Sun Tzu alludes to the story of General Ts'ao in his Art of War, who set up a clear set of melancholic rules; one forbidding injury to fields of crops. One of which he accidentally broke, when his horse wandered into a field of corn, and for which the penalty was execution. His troops loved him and knew that if they lost him that they were in trouble but they could not placate his sense of justice, for he of course stubbornly stuck to the rules. They were eventually able to save his life by some artfully constructed penance (he had to cut off his hair rather than his head), which placated his stubborn sense of justice. Now, I am not advocating different rules for different people. What this story is here to illustrate is the extent of Melancholic stubbornness, for it will even operate against itself with firm principle.

I will stop now, but not because I have run out of complaints. If you wish to get the full rundown on Melancholic faults and complaints, just get the spouse of a Melancholic complaining about their spouse. Look at the way they glance sideways before starting, for the melancholic can hear 1/99th of the story and they fill the rest in seamlessly. Some people would call it being a little suspicious but what would I know?

We all just need to accept that all of our strengths and incredible qualities are the very seat of our weaknesses and we need to understand how our interactions affect those around us, from their perspectives, not ours! That is usually a bitter exercise but if you wish to grow, it is irreplaceable.

Spot the Melancholic

You can tell a Melancholic by their brooding thoughtful attitude, their hatred of mess and disorganisation and the fact that they will most likely be very well dressed. They will be meticulously turned out and love to be well organised. A pure Melancholic must have everything in its place or he is not at all comfortable. The active mind of the Melancholic simply must examine every possibility, from every angle, before coming to a decision. Whatever has to be done must be done perfectly and meticulously. When you find someone who has these qualities, hurrah! You have

found a Melancholic. There will not be too much show, but there will be stimulating conversation if you can manage to loosen their tongue.

Know Yourself

So Why Are You Like This?

The Element Earth and Autumn characterise you. The elemental energies which express themselves in you shape your psychology and physiology. Your behaviour and primal impulses express this. Earth is solid, fixed, rooted and rooting, strong, supporting, containing, maintains shape and is slow to change. Autumn is the retreat of the vegetation which flourished in spring and summer into the bleak, barrenness of winter, the hot dryness of summer loses its heat and the dryness becomes cold ushering in the cold, frozen dampness of winter. Hence, conservation, preparing and calculating worst case scenarios are hardwired into your being. You calculate possibilities and imagine scenarios with an ever present awareness of the threats inherent in living. The energy of action should bring forth a result and so you calculate and imagine internally long before acting.

In keeping with the conservation of energy, you communicate with little expressiveness and gesticulation. Your posture will tend to be closed and protective and you find crowds tiring and difficult. This is just the music that resounds through you. To master your form you must become familiar with the music that sings through you and the way that others hear it. The hotter, more extroverted types, tend to find your communicative conservationism confusing, they can't work out why your signals are so muted. These differences are really worth reflecting upon.

You really don't tell a story, you explain and educate, filling in that which logically supports what appears on the surface. Your communicative habit assumes that when people understand they will change the way that they act, but this is not necessarily the case. In fact it almost always is not the case. Some people may even resent you deeply for opening their eyes, when they are fervently committed to keeping things the same. So you explain and give rational supporting arguments, history and reasons, whys, hows, wherefores, probabilities, permutations, gradations, options, consequences, fomentations, facts (your unreserved favourite), falsehoods and their histories, effects and more. This is your genius. It also means that often you have a genius for losing people along the way in the sheer volume of detail! Mastering this type requires the development of a significant capacity for non-idealistic empathy. You have gained the ability to see things through the eyes of others on their terms, which does not mean that you agree with them, but that you understand why they see the world in the way that they do, accept that it is a valid way of seeing the world and can use that to understand the nature of what confronts us with a lot more clarity than just being stuck with your default outlook.

As you can appreciate with this amount of reflection, calculation and considerations, procrastination seems the logical outcome.

Your type has its strengths and to really benefit from them we just have to commit to loads of self development. The Germans call it Bildung or self-cultivation.

Melancholic Relationships

In relationships you are loyal but you keep account of everything done and that which you do. The more self absorbed or insecure you are is the more that you count. You will be the dependable companion, organising, planning and keeping track. This comes as second nature to you. The more insecure you are and the more you lack self esteem, is the less you trust your impulse to do these things, however stepping back from your natural sphere really doesn't leave you comfortable within yourself. You naturally have to regulate your interactions and you don't show very much emotion. Since you think that having thought through what you do and then doing it then that should be enough for the other party to realise that you care deeply, you just have to realise that different types have very different ways of expressing feelings and building relationships and you must remember that it is necessary to spend some time translating your impulse into an emotional and relationship building language that they can recognise and understand. You don't have to do it all of the time but it is really helpful to speak them in a language that they understand, which then helps them to calibrate their expectations and learn to read your emotional and relationship building language. Remember that you think things through and lack spontaneity whilst Sanguines are spontaneous, Cholerics will scarcely state how they feel forcefully, or they will forcefully let you know by their behavior, and Phlegmatics will stand back and allow you to draw close perhaps occasionally, but spontaneously giving your subtle consistent signals that they care about you and are building a relationship.

Above I am speaking of relationships in general not specifically intimate relationships. Remember that your language seems a bit cold to others and in order to build a relationship (a friendship is a relationship) you need to be able to mutually calibrate and this is where the difficulties lie in relationship building. So, you should also learn to speak about these things with people with whom you have relationships. Getting them to read the series is a very useful aid.

Remember that people need to work things out for themselves, and so, as a Melancholic seeing clearly some matter of difficulty encountered by one of your friends, avoid offering advice that is not requested. It is better to say something like, 'Are you sure that you want to do that?', or, 'Are you sure that you should?', or, 'Have you really thought this through?', or,

'Are you sure that this is the thing to do?'. I have learned the hard way that advice is often not desired or appropriate, and Melancholics as the great thinkers love to offer advice, and as for Cholerics! Cholerics often offer advice in barrages like a battering ram! Anyway, this is not a book about Cholerics. Whenever we can it is a lot better to facilitate someone working it out for themselves, rather than offering them a predigested meal of advice. People need to chew on things for themselves to absorb them well. Asking questions like, 'What do you think is happening here?', or, 'If that happened how would you feel and how do you think they would feel?'. Help them to break their problem or challenge into bits that they can chew on and work out for themselves. Offer access to your Melancholic genius for thinking things through, rather than solutions that have not been specifically asked for. Then you must remember that they may not be Melancholics, and so will chew on the problem in very different ways to you. Mastering facilitation is an incredible skill to perfect, and once you have, life will often be a lot easier and those around you really benefit. Don't crowd out their genius, but rather facilitate its expression and learn from the different natural strategies.

Your natural loyalty and capacity as a historian means that you do things for others and remember what you have done and expect others to remember, and they perhaps do, but no one likes to be frequently reminded of their debt to you. Practice selflessness, and observe how people deal with the things that you have done over time, if they appreciate and benefit from it then do more and if they don't do less. Also supporting those who support others, supports more people, than if we support those who do not. Focusing upon people's behaviour over time gives a much better ability to predict what they will do. There is often an astonishing variance between what people say and what people do and when you meet someone whom behaviour and statement match up to each other, then know that you have found a particularly rare gem.

When you are able to predict people's behaviour in your mind's eye, still remember that they are able to change. However, what we look for is a change which is extended over time. Some people's higher and lower natures are just in conflict and flux and learning to recognise which conditions bring out which is really useful. Some people's anxiety about their provision brings out the worst in them, so avoid dealing with them when it comes to questions of money, wealth and provision in general, and if you give to them then just forget about it. We benefit by treating people according to their natures not according to how we assume they should be.

Remember that your tendency to see problems often causes you to assume the worst in situations and people. This is just your initial tendency but as you will have observed it is not always correct, so let the tendency happen and then observe the problem or challenge from other angles including a few optimistic ones. Then use the pessimistic insights to know what to avoid and the optimistic ones to explore what may be possible. We need to develop healthy relationships with our impulses and to learn that they are often not accurate, learning to increase the accuracy of our predictions and to improve the way that we navigate relationships will yield much better results in the long run than merely allowing our tendencies and impulses to just run riot. This leaves us much more balanced, and makes us surer about our world since we learn how better to navigate it.

You need space to recover your energetic reserves, to reflect upon things and to just decompress. This is an essential need of a Melancholic, so whether your insecurities, or people's crowding into your space drives your lack of personal space, the result will be the same. Your need for space will overwhelm you and you will claim your needed personal space by overturning the situation. Remember that this can often destroy relationships. Because when you desperately need the space, you will invariably disregard the connection between our needs, our actions and the consequences.

Though you need personal space you also need to know where the situation is going and the wait and see attitude scarcely works for you. You need to select your options and to be aware of what the options are.

Stubbornness is problematic, perseverance is virtuous and sticking to clear fundamentals is wisdom. Repeat this again!

Sulking

When you do not get your way, you sulk. You descend into the dark, foreboding, damp, miserable lands of the sulk. With a mastery of this passive aggressive strategy. Just remember that when your sulking ends that the problem often remains. That when we persuade others with our sulking that we reap resentment, and often more sulking results. Sulking doesn't win the argument when it works. When it works it just gets us our way and that comes at a price.

When it doesn't work then the issues still remain. It really is your choice.

Melancholic in Love

Melancholics in love expect devotion. They need to be secure in the fact that they are loved and safe in that love. They are initially suspicious of the love and worry that it will end and so require proof that they are loved and safe. If you love a Melancholic, expect to be tested. Your conversations reflected upon and some cross examination in retrospect to take place. Weeks later when the questions come don't be surprised. Their loyalty means that they wish to give their entire hearts, but their natural wariness demands that they proceed with caution. When they abandon that to dive deeply into love's ocean then they are really deeply in love but expect moments of insecurity for they have dived into an ocean and their natural impulses will rise suddenly and powerfully to the surface. There is a tendency to be either matter of a fact about love, or to construct lovely stories expressing their love ideal. Remember that the matter of fact Melancholic still has a love ideal and that the love ideal dominated Melancholic can still be matter of a fact. If you are in love with a Melancholic, then you would do well to understand their love ideal, and to make clear some of your terms and conditions as you navigate this, for often with Melancholics you will realise after the fact that you have actually entered into an unstated contract, and you would do well to understand what that is and to 'manage expectations'. For Melancholics see detail and they keep detailed accounts and you may find yourself presented with a list of contractual infractions that you had not even realised existed. They will inevitably be things you didn't do and another list of things that you did in the wrong way. It's just part of the pattern and to expect it to be different because you would like it to be, really isn't going to get you anywhere.

As a Melancholic you want to give yourself over to love completely, but your natural wariness encourages you to proceed with caution, and this is natural and even desirable for you. You can tend to really be dominated by ideals, and idealising a person really sets a relationship up for failure. Proceeding with caution really gives you space to see them and to learn to deal with them as they are, and not as you would like them to be, and helps you to proceed at a pace that you are more comfortable with.

You have a romantic love ideal or ideals, and it is important to examine them so that you may

42

understand what motivates you in your love quest. Some love ideals are so idealised that they are utterly impossible to fulfill and an idealised action may be loaded with significance only for you, and may not at all have meaning for the other person. So that when they deliberately fulfil your love ideal, it pleases you but may mean nothing to them, and since what you desire is proof of their devotion, love or loyalty, the action happens but it really doesn't prove anything except the fact that they know what is important to you and so they did it. Whilst this is an important aspect of any relationship, all it really proves is that the person is committed enough that they want to give you what you want. Invest in understanding their love ideal, and also examining your own. See that with people, actions have meaning to them and understanding that about them, helps you to see what they are really saying by their display of love. This helps us to move into a space in which it is possible to translate across love languages and understand what the other may be really saying because of your capacity to empathise with them. This often yields much better results. To be secure you need them to prove their devotion, loyalty and love and this is the deep need, so we need to learn to fulfil this need in the best possible way for the health of our relationships. Often we realise that the ideal isn't healthy and when that happens we can set about changing it.

Judge Dredd The Melancholic Accountant

You keep detailed accounts! You are a relationship historian and the Judge Dredd! Judge Dredd is judge, jury and executioner. You keep your tally and cross examine and draw your conclusions unless you are blinded by an excessive love ideal and you have decided that this person is the ideal, in which case you still keep tally but you will bury it deeply and suppress it when it starts to rise to the surface. In a relationship with a Melancholic you would do well to expect and prepare for cross examinations and expect your actions and intentions to be cross referenced. What keeps you in check Melancholic, when you are in a balanced state is that there will also be some healthy skepticism regarding your conclusions. Thank God!

Insecurity in Relationships

Insecurity in relationships is a natural corollary to your instinctive pessimism. You fear that the worst will happen and so must guard against it.

Since we have established that this is merely your default impulse you have to develop good listening and observation skills in order to learn to map the world as it is and not as your fears would dictate, and it often happens that we construct our world according to our fears. We behave as if the world will confirm our fears and then we act as if that which we fear is present in the world and by that we bring your fearful prophesy into being, confirming our skewed sense of reality. This happens with all people more often than we'd like and it really doesn't have to be that way. Relationships are built upon trust, and trust can either be given or it is earned. Trust which is given establishes a wide range of trusts which are assumed and as they are broken we change our opinion regarding what we may trust that person with. When it is earned we start with an assumption that we do not know what to trust this person with and we learn by responding to their behaviour, trusting what they do and have done as an indication of what to trust them with. There are these two approaches and it seems that the second is most suited to the Melancholic.

A Melancholic Broken Heart

A broken heart is part of human experience and we learn and grow beyond that if we learn to take it in our stride. The great risk of love is losing it. This is always there and so love is really for the courageous and it reveals the deep courageous essence of human beings. We love with the knowledge of its cost always lying beneath the surface. Heartache and heartbreak walk hand in hand with love. A broken hearted Melancholic walls themselves into an impregnable fortress, for the heart having been broken once with the deep pain experienced, they begin to prepare for all eventualities. This lonely, cold, forbidding fortress is a place of foreboding, or else endless activity to distract from the pain in a heart that refuses to move on. If we have the courage to love, then we must also muster the courage to walk through the desolation and destruction of heartbreak, in all of its dark, painfully desolate despair. It will not last, and it will certainly pass. Some of the pain may remain forever. However, the dark, desolate despair will pass. It is here that we must bind our kidneys, straighten our backs, lift our chins, bring our shoulders back and step into the world regardless of the pain. Some of the greatest and most beautiful poetry of heartbreak is by Melancholics striding through this wasteland of despair. Read Nathan McClain's Love Elegy in a Chinese Garden, With Koi.

You would do well to learn to change the manner in which trust is understood. Trust is often understood in the light of an ideal of what people should do. This is rarely ever not disappointed, and this confirms their pessimistic view of human nature. How on earth will other human beings live up to your ideals, when even we can't live up to our own ideals? Human beings don't do what they should do, they do what they do! Circumstances reveal different behavioural possibilities in people. Observe what people do and trust them to do what they do. Trust the pattern that is observed and leave space open for people to reveal themselves. In love this allows us to move beyond loving the idealised person to loving the person warts and all. And perhaps this is why so many Melancholics marry Sanguines!

Melancholic Friend

Turn up for the appointments (I mean dates or days and nights out), they are important. Melancholics dance around an issue when they want to do it and so end up exploring why something isn't a good idea, how it can't be done, what is wrong with something, ... may often mean that this is the thing that the Melancholic wishes to do. Melancholics need friends that may act as a sounding board and help them to unknot their suspicions, fears, worries, desires and other matters in the cauldron of the Melancholic mind by reflective listening. Help them to work things out, encourage them to really revisit what they want to do and most of all aid them in keeping hope and high expectations alive. Your penchant for overthinking will challenge the people who have to listen to you trudge through the detail as you work things out and so they have to be patient. It usually means that you will only have a few close friends and that is ok, for you need quality over quantity and you tend to find too many people tiresome. So, though you like the idea of being popular, you would hate the reality of being surrounded by too many people. Too much attention tends to make you self-conscious and learning to deal with this is a necessary self development goal if you really wish to grow. In that you would do well to learn from Sanguines. In our friends we support ourselves especially with the qualities which we do not naturally possess. We may then learn from them, and them from us. Wit is your natural joking style and you would do well to explore it and develop it. The problem often emerges when your wit becomes rather cruel., Underdeveloped Melancholics often use dry, caustic wit to habitually undermine those by whom they feel challenged,. Developing a secure, healthy, mature sense of self keeps this at bay, or at least in check. Do remember that if this is left unchecked it can actually become quite monstrous. There are, of course, times when people really just deserve it just to keep them under control,, so don't forget the usefulness of this superpower.

Learning to hear your friends out to the end of their arguments and in the different ways that the types unfold their ideas and thoughts is something that Melancholics really need to learn, for the unflappable Melancholic logic and rationality, will often be employed to shut down avenues of thought and exploration which seem stupid to you and in which so much could go wrong. Learn to hear people out and help them to explore their own thoughts, it is often better that they themselves see their own absurdities and issues by examining themselves. Even when they ask for your opinion it is often better to support them in understanding what is deeply embedded in theirs. To do this we have to develop a deep and robust capacity for empathy and conversation, and this is only possible by practising, lots of practice. In short give your friends" thoughts space to breathe on terms that suit them, and not just yours. And remember that after listening and enduring their ideas, that you don't have to agree with them, but by the end you will understand what motivates them much, much better. I guarantee you that you will learn lots this way and that through this you will grow immensely. And becoming more understanding of how others are in the world, forces you to develop. This actually helps you to experience the world as a safer place. Trust me, your friends will appreciate it (Eventually!).

You are always interested in something and this is your superpower. So keep interested in things and pursue this. Your natural friend zone is with those that like to have interests. You find it easy to talk about subjects that you are really interested in and so having interests keeps life and conversation interesting for you and those around you. Your loyalty and penchant for organisation converge well on this and so scheduling in events and involving yourself in them adds nicely to your friendliness quotient. Get a menagerie of different types to fulfil the various roles required to keep things interesting, and make sure that they all have a chance to shine.

As a Melancholic friend beware of becoming resentful. Maintain appropriate boundaries and learn to speak up when your territory has been encroached upon, and do not allow people to habitually invade your territory or to treat you badly, as this will lead you to ruminate over this endlessly, and it usually ends up with the kind of resentment that is often compounded with bitterness. Learn techniques of maintaining boundaries and dealing with people's bad behaviour (it will happen). When Melancholics are resentful your digestion tends to deteriorate and by the time that bitterness takes root you are usually quite ill. Just consider resentment bad for your health. This means that poor boundaries and not keeping people in check, which leads to resentment, are particularly bad for you and your health.

Beware of stinginess and keeping count of what you do for others. It seems that this method of accounting and stinginess is always weighted in favour of the one counting and we tend to overlook what others do for us. I have often seen Melancholics remind others of what they have done for them, which forces the other party to take account of what they have done which has gone unnoticed. This often leads to the other person deciding that the balance of transactions is really not in their favour and this often leads to people breaking off the friendship or just becoming much more aware and readjusting the balance of the relationship. Then we are left to discover the true value what it was we had, but only after we have lost it!

Remember that you tend to bring good sense and grounding to your circle of friends, so be kind, considerate and gentle with it. And remember that though dangers and threats may exist, they won't all happen, and so we often have to guard only against the most dangerous and probable cases, and it is here in the space of how safe you feel in the world that the Melancholic sense of balance is frequently either made or destroyed. You have to commit to doing the work that nourishes that sense of self, place in the world and sense of security, for your superpowers to really shine.

Invest In Relationships

If you are reading this because you have a Melancholic friend who perpetually sees all of the hurdles, the dangers and the best way to do everything, here is a tip. Melancholics find it really difficult to dwell in the present and will tend to be historians or to look too far into hypothetical futures. Really focusing upon the present and the possibilities that this opens to us now is a natural antidote to their speculations of the dangers ahead. They are trying to save you from yourself and the dangers that you might expose yourself to. You will have to limit the conversation firmly and gently to the present possibilities, and to discuss these. Remind them that it is ultimately your decision and you have a very different relationship with risk to theirs. With time they will begin to learn what types of risk you are comfortable with. But good luck with dealing with this one!

Melancholic At Work

Work must be interesting and intellectually stimulating. Some Melancholics will often do something routine in order to have the space to do something intellectually stimulating e.g becoming a librarian so that they can read books. The Melancholic likes to solve puzzles and put things in order. You need space to work things out and so working alone works for you. Because you don't have a problem with routine, doing work that engages your capacity for routines works. However, your need for intellectual stimulation and challenge is always present and activities will become frustrating if this capacity of yours is not engaged.

The challenge of the Melancholic is procrastination. You want perfection and to cover all the weaknesses or at least the major weaknesses (but who defines the major weaknesses?). You procrastinate and may end up with unfinished open projects waiting for some perfect part to be completed. Because the idea of the thing is sometimes more important to you than the actual thing, you may end up waiting for something that you don't actually need, or doesn't make the critical difference to the project. Prototyping is a useful methodology for you whenever this is possible. Build the minimum that the thing needs to work. It may have reduced functionality and may not meet all of the requirements, but it will get you into the zone of how the thing really works, how it is used and when and where it is really deployed. This then allows you to improve based upon a real grasp of the thing. Of course, there are many instances where this is not an appropriate methodology. However, applying the principles you will have learned will aid you in adjusting your approach.

Your creative approach employs puzzle like problem solving and building solutions in stages. You need time to work things out and order them. You need to solve the creative problem. Which is very different to the approaches of the wetter types; i.e. the sanguine and phlegmatic. You really need periods without interruption to order your thoughts and to develop solutions creatively.

Dealing with people and socialisation is often difficult for you and accepting and working with this weakness can actually turn it into a major strength.

Melancholics who are ill or chronically stressed may often seek a protective bubble of routine and will often avoid variety and experimenting with new things. This will not serve the Melancholic well and will aggravate your illnesses, anxiety and stresses. You must find ways of engaging with some variety and change. This will help you to keep your balance.

6 Ways of Dealing With Procrastination

1. Procrastination isn't always a bad thing! Well, responding inappropriately to the impulse to procrastinate is always a bad thing. Knowing how to use the impulse to wait when waiting is required makes waiting for the right moment easier. Timing is often everything. By this I mean waiting and preserving your resources until the circumstances are most favourable is a virtue. You know that you're getting this

right when you can wait and then act at the time deemed appropriate without hesitation. This is called developing timing. The disciplines of timing such as waiting, observing, understanding the fundamentals and rhythms of what needs to be done are skills to be developed and perfected. Then at times we will get it wrong and this is expected, for judgment improves by error and successes, both being necessary to develop the ability to judge when a course of action is appropriate.

2. Keep someone close, to whom you have given permission to nag you whenever you procrastinate. This arrangement must be by agreement, and the person should take note of the signs of how you procrastinate, and reflect that back to you when it is appropriate to discuss your procrastination. This will make you squirm but you will learn a great deal about yourself. For this to work you have to work at not lashing out or sulking, both these things will happen but having agreed to the terms of engagement then you can apologise and make amends afterwards. This is important because by making amends and apologising you are punishing your own bad behaviour. For this to work you will have to keep making

amends until they accept your apology. Good luck!

3. Everyday do something small that needs to be done without delaying it. You are building anti-procrastination muscle. Keep them small and increase the weight gradually. Have a good laugh at the kinds of arguments and justifications that you come up with and then do what needs to be done anyway.

4. Schedule things and set deadlines. Penalise yourself with pushups or some other type of exercise when you don't stick to schedule.

5. Reward yourself when you stick to schedule. Reward yourself when you don't procrastinate.

6. Make sure that you get sufficient sleep and rest. Melancholics really procrastinate when they are tired.

5 Ways of Doing New Things

Most Melancholics find too much change difficult and love routine. The problem is that though you love routine you also love stimulation and fresh differences and their challenges are often the way that you will receive this. So you love stimulation but like the familiar, and a bored Melancholic is miserable. Without new challenges you will become rigid and inflexible and develop a range of rules as to how things should be done and what needs to be where. Then you become really difficult to live with! Boredom really doesn't bring out the best in you.

Why don't we come to a compromise? You should try something new every week and do the work, contributing to it daily during that week, just in order to get better at it. Study your reactions to new things, especially the reasons you might find for not doing them. See how your self works when it is forced to squirm, when facing something new, and learn to have a giggle about it with yourself. You can even come up with some jokes that you can tell to those who really know you. Ah! and if you are interested you can even learn how to tell jokes well.

Here are 5 ways of doing new things:

1. Set a day of the week to start your new things challenge, and set aside some time to do it. Of course, the first thing that will happen is that you will decide that there are more important things to do, than to do something as pointless as this! If this one gets you three times in a row, then you are really getting to grips with what it means to be a Melancholic!

2. Choose fun things for the first three months. Yes, fun things! What is the point? The point is that it is fun!

3. Celebrate your success. In this case please don't punish the failure to get this task done. Just focus upon celebrating the successes. Please!

4. Set a reminder. A great Melancholic strategy is to conveniently forget. We know that this isn't a pretence at forgetting. Melancholics forget and sometimes it can also become a useful excuse, once you figure out that you sometimes forget.

5. Every month do something new with other people, this is for fun and relaxation. It helps to make it the kind of thing during which your Melancholic strengths are useful and well appreciated.

Good luck with all this! I would love to hear your stories!

The Melancholic at Play

You love rules, methods, practices, understanding and exploring rules, and understanding rules, and options and features and ... Yes that's just the way that you're wired. On the other hand, the Choleric needs to win, the Sanguine to abandon to sensation and have fun, the Phlegmatic to observe, surprise and keep their options open. You want to play for a reason, and if you must win, it is to prove your superior grasp of the rules of the game. You will master the game and there are times when play becomes a work of calculation.

Play for you isn't just leisure, this doesn't seem to motivate you, and this is characteristic of the dry types. The dry types are focused upon an objective, the goal for you and your Choleric cousin, is more important than the journey (yes I do know how irritating you find Cholerics). The challenge for you is that you need leisure, and so you have to balance your need for leisure with your need to work at understanding the game. Leisure has to have enough fun or we just don't survive the activity for the time needed to master it. The mind, like a muscle, becomes tired. In Unani Tibb (Hippocratic Medicine amongst Muslims) we say that the mind eats the body. The mind is energy hungry, and especially in the Melancholic, is given priority over the rest of the body for energy resources. As a Melancholic at play you have to learn to make it fun. Sanguines and Phlegmatics really have something to teach you here, for they are capable of an abandon which doesn't come naturally to you. Sometimes the way to understand is to come at it from the underneath, so to speak. To give way to abandon, and wander into its experiential centre, is never going to come naturally to you, just understanding that there are other ways of orienting ourselves to knowledge and that immersion grants us insights that do not come to those who don't immerse themselves. Melancholics may find that acquiring an ability for true leisure, actually speeds up their learning and mastery. Melancholics like abstraction as this allows for very neat and understandable organisation of our world. However, the messiness of real life really isn't quite like that and this capacity for immersion allows the development of the capacity to build much more accurate maps of the real world. For the Melancholic leisure holds great secrets and opportunities for self-development.

When playing in groups, you and the Cholerics would do well to let the Sanguines take charge, and if you are feeling particularly courageous let the Phlegmatics do so. If they know how to do so well then they will literally blow your minds. From these two types you will learn the art of making the journey fun. Control and directedness can sometimes be over rated.

Melancholic Thought

The tops are at the top, the bottoms are at the bottom. The inside is the inside, and the outside is not the inside, and the inside is not the outside. The natural order of your minds and its capacity to make order of the messiness of the world is just legendary. Melancholics will come at the messy, chaotic nature of the world with minds that find order in the world. Melancholics impose an order upon the world so that it corresponds with their well made conceptual maps. This is the genius of the Melancholic, but the mind map is not the terrain, and so the great genius of the Melancholic may also become an impediment for them..

Melancholics make paradigms, mental terrain maps, and love to solve the puzzles which explore the paradigm. So, whilst they explore the paradigm with astounding mental dexterity and creativity, they can tend to avoid leaving the paradigm, surrounding their uncanny flexibility with an inflexibility that can be shocking. Melancholics love solving puzzles and figuring out intellectually connected ways of finding solutions. Melancholics literally engineer solutions to problems or puzzles, and so they will be found wherever these skills are in demand. They are innovative and at the same time inflexible. Contradiction? Well that's in the nature of the messiness of the world.

For Melancholics they would do well to learn that there are two vastly different methods of thought; the Inductive and the Deductive. Melancholics find deductive reasoning very easy. Deductive reasoning allows emotional distance, abstraction and detailed relational maps, whilst Inductive reasoning requires immersion, the view from the messy middle, and letting the maps emerge rather than be confined to the path of abstraction. For truly masterful intellectual development if we develop a capacity to appreciate and negotiate both ways of thinking, we develop a flexibility rarely seen with either wet or dry types. It allows us to appreciate a world beyond our paradigm and to realise the arbitrariness of our paradigms. Great minds don't necessarily think alike, Melancholic!

The mind of the Melancholic's takes precedence over their digestion. Your powerful minds digest your world at the expense of your capacity to digest your food. This is useful for Melancholics to remember, because they possess weak digestion and a day of mental exertion followed by a really heavy meal can literally be a nightmare for Melancholics. A great mind comes at a price!

The Nine Tips For Melancholic Socialising

1. So you are naturally suspicious and this isn't really news. So just allow yourself sufficient time and space to get to know people. When you first meet them it helps if you don't face them head on, and you should expect things to be a little awkward to start off. Also, try to have tiered boundaries because when you meet people you need to see who they are and to decide how close you want them to get to you. Don't assume that they all have to be close friends. There are:

- Acquaintances - People you know and occasionally meet, but they aren't friends they are just people you know. You're probably asking yourself why. View this as a holding pen for people that you've just met.

- Friends - These people are just friends. You meet and perhaps occasionally do things together. You meet socially with other friends and they provide a safe group to travel with. You don't need to engage in long conversations with them.

- Closer Friends - These are people you will meet more regularly and do things together regularly. You know that they look out for you, and you look out for their interests too.

- Close Friends - These are people who you hold close and whom you trust.

- Bosom Buddies - Self explanatory.

2.   Start people in the first tier and keep your distance, but be polite. When you speak to them don't face them head on. In other words, don't let their centre line face yours, it's just uncomfortable for Melancholics. Keep your centre line facing off centre, and turn your head slightly so that you can look them in the eye or break eye contact as and when it suits you. This also conveys the clear impression that you don't mind talking, but with no intention of getting too close. If you are dealing with a bombastic choleric then fold your arms tightly and turn your feet away from them. This will start to send the right message. Keep initial meetings short and always have in reserve good reasons to leave. Decide whether you want to be friends. You might Facebook friend them but you won't give them your number.

3.   People who you allow closer as Friends are just friends. You don't need to answer their calls when they call you and can text them

back instead, with a, 'Sorry I missed your call ...' message and can keep the exchange to text messages. When you meet deal with them based upon how comfortable you are. People are different and you don't need to be falling over yourself to be too friendly. You never meet them alone and keep the Friends tier to group interactions.

4. Closer Friends are those who you meet with in small groups and whom you would occasionally eat out with in small gatherings. It is easier to keep this group to those with whom you share clear interests with.

5. Close Friends are those who you would visit and perhaps stay with, or invite to stay overnight, or even travel with alone. You can talk to each other with relative ease and you know how they are, what they want, and how they tend to react. Yes, they may surprise you, but you know them well enough to be able to relax. For Melancholics this takes time, often it could be years.

6. Bosom Buddies. This just happens with time.

7. Work at understanding Close Friends and closer ones. Understand who they are, what motivates them, and why. Listen to them,

ask questions and find out about the things that interest them and that interest you. This makes interesting conversation easier, and when they say something that you might think stupid, just hold your opinions and find out why they said it, what they intend, and how they are about those things. Listen more to the answers and use the opportunity to understand people.

8. Always have an exit strategy for social interactions that are particularly exhausting. Keep a bank of effective,, well rehearsed exit strategies. After you've noticed the third sign that you should leave, then don't hesitate, it is time to leave.

9. Remember that suspicion is just suspicion, and Melancholics tend to expect the worst, but that's ok. Being prepared for the worst is not a bad thing, but the Melancholic reflex is not reality and so NOT learning to distinguish between Melancholic suspicion and what is really happening is a major problem. We are alive and so the worst rarely happens, so make excuses for people. Though you may expect the worst, acknowledge when this is not the case, and just remind yourself that most times suspicion is unfounded. Melancholics need to practice keeping suspicion in its proper

place. Give people the benefit of the doubt, ask questions and let things become clear before acting on suspicion.

Yes, socialising is difficult for Melancholics, so don't feel obligated to behave as if it is not. Remember that they are not you, and that other types don't necessarily think things through before speaking, as Melancholics do.

Melancholic Learning and Study Style

Melancholics are either awkward mavericks or conformists. There is very little meeting in between. They have a studious eye and a good memory for detail. We are all drawn to what we love and Melancholics are in love with detail. Dear Melancholic, just ask your friends. Your love of detail isn't an infatuation, it's a raving love affair! When learning make full use of this superpower. Quickly construct a scaffolding of the knowledge area and then let your passion for detail take over. Curiosity also drives you, so in a patchwork which raises many questions for you, learn to ride your natural inclinations to learning success. The scaffolding can be dates of significant events, stages of development, stages of chemical change, psycho-social development stages. Create tensions between note taking styles, if you like note taking in sketches then, mix in words, rhyming phrases, draw on pictures, remember the faces of prominent figures and use this to build a layered, playful picture of the area that you are studying, loaded with areas pregnant with curiosity and questions, lots of questions, Melancholics love questions. Now, really use your love of detail to build knowledge maps that you can sit back, close your eyes and imagine. Reach up and touch things to activate that living visual memory and imagination, move things around and explore connections and questions. Read biographies, and go madly deep. Melancholics love to be treasure troves of information, understanding and insight. Use it and use it well.

Now, there is studying for a qualification or a job, and there is studying for our own interests. Staying on track for qualifications with passion is often difficult for Melancholics, you study for the qualification and get good grades often with very little passion and deep interest, or you chase your own interests with Melancholic passion (yes I know that you other types wouldn't want to call it 'passion' but it is, it just isn't outwardly expressed in the way that you'd expect).

If you want to keep your life interesting and passionate you will have to find your balance.

Otherwise, you'd best choose an area that you are simply fascinated with. But this tension will always remain.

How to present your work. Now, that is true terror for a Melancholic.

Melancholic Decision Making

At this point, I would like to offer all of my Melancholic readers a sincere apology. This title is a contradiction in terms. What is Melancholic Decision Making? Procrastination?

Melancholic Decision Making looks like this. You lay out and explore every possible option, permutation, choice, non-choice, condition, change in condition, what could go wrong and what can't go right. Then you proceed to punish yourself by going over them repeatedly, just in case you missed something, then over again to ensure that you didn't miss anything. Then you discuss the details with those around you who will listen, if you are the voluble type. Then you narrow it down to some likely options and then doubt whether you chose the correct options and check them all again. If you're tired, it's even worse. Then you worry about taking a decision in case you make the wrong one and then you check your options again, worry that the conditions have changed and check them again. So then the decision is left as

70

close to the deadline as you can leave it whilst you constantly go back and forth. Melancholic decision making is a torturous business. Will things go wrong? Of course, they always do!

By now, the Melancholic has forgotten that they are still quite alive, they have eaten for a few days in succession, bathed, travelled and generally lived in a world where everything that could go wrong goes wrong. It has all gone so wrong that they are living fairly well, until the present and that next breath of air that they are about to breathe has somehow managed to reach them. It really is a miracle for the Melancholics that they can maintain this pessimistic outlook despite these hourly accidental happenings that manage to keep them alive and well! So now, the Melancholic has finally made their decision, and is now worrying that things won't work out, whilst they continue, nevertheless, to work out. At this rate an ulcer might be the desirable thing (Melancholics like to talk about their medicines and illnesses).

Dear Melancholic, can you imagine what life must be like for those who have to live with you whilst you go through all of this? Heaven help us! By now, even a Phlegmatic would be begging and praying for a Choleric to turn up instead.

7 Steps to Successful Decision Making

1. Everything that can go wrong won't. Some things will likely go wrong, but likelihood is not the same as certainty. Write down your options, the risks, opportunities and benefits, dump it on paper, or IPad or whatever, and get it out of your head. Then rank them in order of the worst risk and most benefit, and then look at what you would do if the worst happens.

2. Look at action triggers. These are events, contexts and circumstances which really make the decisions on which of these options are best fitted to the circumstances. An example would be that you're planning a walk in the countryside and there are 10 possibilities, but on windy days 2 of these options would work best, whilst on sunny days 4 of them would offer shade, whilst on warm days 1 ends with a swim and so on, so depending upon the weather your options are narrowed down.

3. Now choose a top 3 based upon what you know and keep your choices strongly dependent upon the circumstances.

4. If you were going to discuss your decision with others to seek advice, now would be a good time. Use this opportunity to hear and

listen to what others have to add to what you know, but keep yourself grounded by considering context and appropriateness and resist the temptation to be abstract and to descend into if this and if that. The more tired you are the more circular this activity will become. So now, you can update your 3 choices.

5. Now you are in a position to choose and you can do this in two ways. The first is that if the weather is sunny, which option would you take,? If it is windy, which option? etc., so that depending upon the trigger or circumstance, the circumstance dictates the choice. The second is that you opt for one choice from the updated 3 choices, but that is harder for a Melancholic.

6. A Melancholic mind naturally generates doubt and so the challenge is to develop a reality principle which can handle this, allowing you to identify doubt and anxiety about decisions that is just background noise which should be ignored, and when the doubt and anxiety are about real possibilities that should be considered. The point of performing points 1 and 2 is that you can update your notes and follow the procedure. This will force you to develop a robust truth principle.

7. Now that you have a decision, and the doubt and anxiety continue to plague you, these postural principles help you to deal with it in a better manner. If you hang your head forward and look downwards it gets worse, and if you look up at the sky and are more upright they lessen their activity. So you've made a decision. Now head off, have a walk and reward yourself with some relaxation, or just move on and do something else.

Decisions

Decision making is difficult for Melancholics, there is a natural background presence of doubt and a natural need to weigh up options. This process is reminiscent of the role of the kidneys which separate the dross from the blood, weighing up the mineral content and swapping out and putting back Sodium, Potassium and other minerals from the blood back into the bloodstream, this for excretion and that for reabsorption. Through the convoluted tubules of the nephrons of the kidneys, keeping track of blood pressure secreting hormones and substances into the blood, initiating chains of regulatory processes which affect the tone throughout the body. Melancholics are like this, they weigh up, balance, conserve, consider regulation, scarcity and future possibilities. Perhaps surprisingly, it is the energy of the kidneys that the Melancholic must guard, particularly the adrenals and hydration dependent functions. Melancholics must rest, they need to go to bed early for all of this weighing, calculation and considering takes its toll and as we say in Greco-Arab Medicine, the mind eats the body!

Melancholic Communication

Time! Melancholics need time to communicate. They think things through before they say them and they weigh the words carefully. This is just how they're wired. If you are in a hurry when communicating with a Melancholic then just remember that their idea of fast may just be your impression of slow, and their idea of slow may just be intolerable, and that is how they are. They may start a sentence, then be struck by a question within it, shift gear internally to answer the question, to their own satisfaction and then resume the sentence. A Melancholic thinks things through with a mind that needs order and linear connections. You will ask, 'What do you think?' ,'What would happen if?,' 'Have you considered?' And because they are about thought and they value thought, will ask these questions with thought in mind. It is an almost foolproof way to spot Melancholics, it's a dead giveaway.

So when communicating with a Melancholic give them time, and Melancholic, when communicating with other types, empathise with them and speak to the type in question from their standpoint. Cholerics need pace, not detail, and want to get to the point. Phlegmatics are about the feel and they want the feel, the intuition and the point, in this way they are rather like Cholerics, but for very different reasons. On the other hand, the Sanguine needs a story, for this is what joins up the thoughts and activates the memory for them. For effective communication we have to remember whom we are communicating with. Remember that you have a penchant for detail and it isn't always necessary. Yes, there are times when the other types come to the Melancholic precisely for detail, but if it is the price they must always pay to communicate with you, then there comes a point at which it seems too costly a price to pay. We have to dance harmoniously with each other.

4 Points To Successful Communication

Melancholics must explain why and must give the granular detail of how, when, where, by how much or how little. Detail, detail, detail, detail, detail, detail.

1. Work at giving the detail that people ask for and just enough. I would just keep repeating this one. Explain when they ask and check before you explain. Most people complain or find this aspect of Melancholics difficult and often it can seem to be condescending. We know that you feel the need to explain and give details so that people understand the how, where and why. But many times they don't need to know, and Cholerics who really don't do unnecessary detail (yes you really differ with them on this one), don't tend to appreciate being forced to listen to your lengthy explanations as they wait for you to give them the essentials, and they will become impatient and they will interrupt you.

2. Speak to people where they are. Speaking to them where they are enables connection and the point of successful communication is to connect. Phlegmatics empathise and focus on feelings, so speaking to them from that perspective can really help you to connect with them. Sanguines need stories and feelings, and you need to get to the point, and it has to be fun. Cholerics just get

to the point quickly, and only tell them what they've asked for. If you need to explain it helps to say to Cholerics, 'Look you're asking me a question that requires explanation and if you want me to answer that then you're going to get an explanation.'

3. Cholerics will interrupt you, so don't take it personally, and they are a bit brash. It's not personal, it's just Cholerics. Phlegmatics prefer to listen and they won't engage with you unless they want to, if you push it, they will tend to just remain evasive and won't connect, they don't have something against you, they are just Phlegmatics. Sanguines are like butterflies and if it isn't interesting they disconnect and connect with something that catches their attention and they don't like to keep doing the same thing repeatedly. When the sanguine butterfly flies off, disconnect and keep your centre they will often circle back around.

4. A true conversation is discovery and revelation. In a true conversation you get to meet someone speaking to you from their unknown creative centre. To do so we have to ask questions and tease out what is hidden in them. Our assumptions prevent discovery and they interrupt revelation. So,

learn to listen, to ask questions, to uncover our assumptions and theirs. We must master the art of making clear the lines that we unintentionally draw and learn how to speak beyond them. That is the true, deep art of communication and mastering that is a lifetime's work.

How to Work Out What They Really Want to Know

Try asking! You're a Melancholic really working at not explaining away everything and overloading your audience with detail. Now you want to know what you should really be telling them. Don't worry about what you shouldn't tell them (couching problems negatively is a Melancholic trait). Think about what you should be telling them. To get started try asking them what they want to know. If you ask,,then stick to telling them what they said they wanted to know, but confirm it. Say something like, 'So you would like to know, '...'. Then if they look at you with a confused stare, and confirm that they didn't understand then now, they have asked for it and 'BOOM!', give it to them.

Explain, break it down, but stay focussed upon what they really need to know to make the matter clear and no more. Keep asking. Get people to confirm their understanding by sharing what they've understood.

Melancholic In Company

Rumaisa walked briskly across the train station tarmac. She was well dressed, as always. Her navy blue suit, hung neatly about her slim frame, and the muted but pleasantly earthy scent of her perfume, seemed coordinated to project a quiet sense of style. She pushed her spectacles up her nose and squeezed her index finger further into her book as she marked the page that she had just been reading. She struck an elegant figure, her dark colours making her seem taller than she was. She arrived on the platform for her train with exactly 5 minutes to spare, as she always did. You could set your watch by her, and the man in the dark Armani suits usually did. He had been trying to catch her eye but being a Melancholic also, his signs were too muted to allow Rumaisa to be sure, and Rumaisa had been watching him for the past year. Rumaisa's burning interest was also too muted to allow him to be sure. Ah! There he was. He smiled and fidgeted and Rumaisa smiled and looked away. He mustered the courage to say good night, the first thing he had said to her in a year, Rumaisa replied cordially, wishing him a good night. He asked her what she was reading, and they had a short, slightly awkward, conversation about the book. This would continue for the following month, He would say good night and ask her what she was reading, but they never mustered the courage to ask each other's names.

Melancholics take a long time to become comfortable with others. Expect there to be muted expressions, lots of apologies, unfinished sentences, assumptions, some healthy suspicion and mixed signals. A Melancholic wants to be friends with you and then worries that you might not reciprocate and then after blowing hot just suddenly blows cold. Other types find this confusing and drives them mad. But this can also be a mark of the Choleric and maybe, just maybe, it's a common trait within the Dry types. We have to offer Melancholics consistency, until some comfort and trust emerges, but it just takes time. Now, remember that the signs of friendship and even intimacy of the Melancholic can be quite muted, so that they can quite easily misinterpret a Sanguine's friendliness for romantic interest. That's just the way that people are wired. We get the sweet with the bitter and the bitter with the sweet. And if you want people to be what they are not, then I wish you the best of luck.

7 Uses of Being in Company

Yes, it is tiring, but:

1. Use it to study people. Phlegmatics do people watching as a pastime. Melancholics can people watch too, but this wouldn't or couldn't be a pastime. That just won't work for the Melancholic. But as a way to understand people, to grasp why they are as they are? What makes them tick? Now, is that a worthy enough pursuit? Well to do that you will really have to refine your social skills and develop some skills that just don't naturally fall into your toolkit.

2. You know that Melancholics get lonely and then the question becomes whether it is worth enduring the socialising minefield to enjoy some company. There actually is a solution, but you won't like it. Get out with some regularity, with company that you enjoy. Now a lot is relative. A Sanguine might get out almost every day of the year, the Choleric most days of the week, the Melancholic a few times a month and a Phlegmatic? Well I will leave that to your acute powers of observation.

3. It takes you a long time to build up the trust and comfort of friendships, so you have to invest some time in that, or it won't happen.

4. It is a chance to develop social and people skills. View it as a muscle and give it some exercise.

5. Invest some time learning to listen like a Phlegmatic, to tell stories like a Sanguine and to build boundaries like a Choleric.

6. Join a club based on a community of common interests in order to build peer networks that reinforce the behaviours, skills and knowledge that you want to embody. This accelerates learning via social reinforcement. It could be learning to play a game, a history society, walking clubs or even exercise.

7. Join a public speaking club or group and learn to do effective public speaking, especially learn to tell jokes. Then you will be able to speak in public, tell jokes and socialise to gather more joke making material.

Melancholic Melancholy

Yes, this is a thing! As a Melancholic, you have a strong mind and not the strongest body. This is the luck of the draw, you are strong in one thing and weak in the other. You expand in one direction and contract in the other. You push down to jump up and you must come down to the ground to jump again. You have to take care of that body, often when run down you will suffer from Melancholia or depression. Yes, there are often other reasons, but eliminate rest and self care, and if there are other reasons remember not to neglect rest and self care because these are very important factors in your psychological and physical health. When we were likening the Melancholic to the kidney, we explored this. Go back and read that and really take good stock for your life. Think of yourself as a racehorse of the mind, and treat your racehorse like a thoroughbred.

Now, since you are primed to see the dark side of the cloud you need energy to continue on to the bright side of that very cloud. So investing in your energy, is investing in your psychological balance. Some types start bright and need to discover the darkness, whilst you start dark and need to discover the brightness. Just forcing yourself into positive thinking just misuses your superpower. You tend to start dark, so trust yourself and continue until you come out on the bright side, but don't forget the darkness and the dangers, which you naturally make preparations for. And why do you prepare for these eventualities? This is precisely, because you start by looking at the problems, challenges and dangers. So, if they don't like your 'negative attitude', then that is their problem. The problem comes when you get stuck there, and if you do step back, rest, recover and refocus.

9 Ways Of Dealing With Melancholic Melancholia

1. Don't over-socialise, it is exhausting, and if overdone your psychological defence mechanisms will kick in. Social anxieties and depression often arise and get in the way of your socialising abuse. Remember that loneliness can sometimes do similar things to all of us, so the point is to find your balance and then discover your sweet spot.

2. Go to bed early. I myself suffered for years with back troubles and developed simple exercises to treat my back problems, and I also went for regular treatment. Years later I started going to bed early, and then earlier than I thought I needed to, and to my surprise my back troubles disappeared miraculously. If I regularly go to bed late they return as miraculously as they disappeared. Melancholics in particular need regular habits. Especially sleep habits, and early to bed is an important part of that.

3. Take an adaptogenic tonic. Adaptogenic tonics strengthen hormonal systems and increase your capacity to handle stress.

4. Distress! As a Melancholic you are already a natural worrier and that is a stressor. Reducing your stress load ensures that you don't overexert your underlying systems by just stressing them too regularly. So just regularly working at reducing stress really helps.

5. Exercise and choose stresses that build up capacity. See this as building stress muscle. A naturally weaker body can become much stronger but you've got to invest in the work.

6. Have a close circle of friends who you can be with when you are in Melancholia and they will give you the space and leave you alone. They let you hideout, allowing you to recognise that you have very different needs, but remember that this will only work over time if there is reciprocity.

7. Travel and take holidays. You need regular resets.

8. If you can, ensure that you choose a profession that you can be passionate about, and that engages your natural

genius. An intellectually under stimulated Melancholic, is usually miserable.

9. Find ways of making life interesting by engaging yourself from within. This doesn't depend upon others to define your role. Engage in the way that you want to engage and if you want a fighting chance at success then go to bed early!

Melancholic Impulses

Earth is the element of the Melancholic. It expresses its deep energetic nature through them. Earth is dark, solid, fixed and strong. We build houses, roads, planes (metal and minerals are of the Earth), bodies are constructed from it and it gives structure everywhere. Then hidden within Earth is tremendous life and it sustains both animals and plants by its structure, such that it is often forgotten. The teaming of life within the Earth is so often a thing forgotten, but within each square metre of Earth in healthy living soil, are millions of microbes, animals, fungi and other forms of life, transmuting minerals into organic chemicals drawn through the cycle of life. Then deep within the depths of our Earth lie other minerals; iron, aluminium, manganese, titanium, and many, many others, all hard, cold and dry, which we use for many things, as conductors, for construction, but always to provide structure, a way that things may pass, which is still structure and by which we may build and realise our dreams.

Perhaps in much of this lies the secret of the Melancholic. For Melancholics, muted expression and frequently quiet, withdrawn natures like the Earth, hide great depth, strength and benefit. Melancholic, you ignore this at your peril and to your inestimable loss. You are deep and drawn to depth and this is just how you are made. Any attempt to become shallow simply will not work. It will leave you dissatisfied and unfulfilled. That which provides structure must provide for future needs based upon historical uses and known and established needs, and that's what you are like. You look forward by looking back, like the mythical Akan Sankofa Bird, and you always strive to make the future both understandable and predictable. This is simply how you are made. Often you will clash with other types because you are preparing for threats which they are yet to perceive, and if they do, they feel that you should be more positive about it and to you, this smacks of denial. You look for threats and that is simply your nature. Bringing this into the realm of appropriateness is your perennial challenge. Your balance is attained by ensuring that balance in these matters is maintained. I call this developing your reality principle. This is the development of a remarkable discipline of mind which is able to weigh up the threats and dangers you perceive, in the light of your world, your experience in the world and the advice of those whose insight and foresight you trust. Melancholics must especially remember that no man is an island.

So you are drawn to see and establish structure, and to do this you see regular pattern, whilst the Sanguine may look for the irregularity of pattern, which they may immerse themselves in whilst you are drawn to stand apart and to abstract so that idealism is something that you must be particularly careful of. Developing a penchant for immersing yourself into reality, into what really happens is an important practice for your growth and balance. You require regularity. Regularity of sleep patterns, meals, weekly rhythm, are all particularly important for your balance, so you have to also regularly schedule chaos. For the universe is manifest in opposites and Order and Chaos are twins, who hide the reality of their other twin within them. You have to surprise yourself and regularly submit yourself to that which challenges you and draws you out of your comfort zone, if you wish to grow, thrive and create. Regularity and preparation are your watchwords but spontaneity must be made to live there too.

You do not naturally have great physical energetic reserves, for your mind takes priority over your body in allocation of the choicest available resources and for this reason your internal world is particularly rich and active. Unlike the Sanguine, you are able to explore your hidden depths with thoroughness in which you are outdone only by the Phlegmatic. Your capacity to explore your living, inward meaning world, and your tendency to see threat means that you are often plagued by self-doubt. Self-doubt, however, is your friend. If you engage it with a strong reality principle you will develop a depth of self belief which will shock and surprise you, but this is not an easy path. On your way to it you will be frozen by procrastination and decision freezes but if you trust and continue you will develop a deep, vast, rooted wisdom, which the other types will naturally depend upon and consult. Self-doubt and Self belief are two twins like Order and Chaos and we must learn to make use of them. We must make them serve us by making ourselves submit to the way they are and what they actually teach us.

Self-doubt is our fear speaking to us eloquently, it speaks our weaknesses, our deep anxieties and it is precisely there that we find the path to refining ourselves. Then Self belief gives us the path to the development of appropriateness for we see that the fear and threat do not always align in the world and the Threat and Opportunity are two twins which speak the same reality and Self-doubt teaches us to prepare for the threat such that it becomes an opportunity and the Self belief gives us the centred-ness to surf the wave of the opportunity and to emerge with a capacity for immersion in the opportunity that can even surprise a Sanguine. Our society exalts the extroverts, whilst standing upon the world built in its everydayness by introverts. Don't let that insanity distract you from your overflowing genius.

With people you need time to become comfortable and familiar with them. Use it and don't rush in where fools readily tread. There is an aspect to you which lends itself easily to the approach of wisdom, so make use of it.

Success isn't determined by how many times you win, but by how you play the week after you lose.

-- Pele

The Mixes

Introduction

The Melancholic embodies Elemental Earth, that of structure and stability. We find that this is hard and inflexible. The qualities of the different phenomena classified under Elemental Earth vary in flexibility, hardness and fixedness by the presence of the other Elemental Elements within them. This is why in Ayurveda we find that Kapha includes the drier earthy types and the watery ones. For earth always give structure, and structure is necessary for watery flexibility. Perhaps this is why in Ayurveda the more watery types are included with what we would classify the more dry, earthy types.

Elemental Air, Water and Fire will enter this Earthy species and bring forth its inwardly expressed qualities in surprising ways. For Earth provides structure from which the other Elements may leap forth and express themselves fused through the Elemental Earth.

Form and pattern are transcribed by Elemental Earth, such as the DNA, a double helix of patterned code, which gives pattern to the eventual emergence of proteins, and the deep rhythmicity of biological form. John Coltrane's great contribution of the scalar (in musical terms) tonal nature of reality (which he corresponded with Einstein about) indicates a reality that Pythagoras before him also spoke about. There is this underlying connectedness which dictates that change in one aspect of a form is tonally related to other aspects and having emerged, only certain other scales can emerge, setting clear eras and phases to the dance of creation. This aspect of how the pattern of unfolding is, emerges from Melancholics who are blessed with being able to speak this rhythmicity in rational terms. They speak it as puzzles, often in unintentional riddles and excel in its mathematical form. Perhaps this is why Thelonious Monk (a Melancholic) said, "All musicians are subconsciously mathematicians".

Anyone who hears Schopenhauer or Bach may feel the deep mathematical musicality of their compositions. Schopenhauer said, "Music is not the representation of ideas, but rather of the will itself." And it is here that we see a key to understanding the fabric of existence within a frame, cultural context and a language that we may understand in our time. For true music speaks the will, it is heard and connected, and because our civilisation possesses a collective will, individually expressed in each of us. We must be very careful how we make use of this gift. For the Sufis this is the Divine Will lent to us, and that we must answer in judgement for how we have used it when we return to the Divine. This answering we perpetually do in the fabric of consequence and which we will uniquely do on The Day of Judgement. This expresses the music of existence, and we are active players in it. Jazz in this sense speaks the autonomy of our own improvisation against the imprisonment within the establishment of what became a Classical unchangeable form, as an imperial project of imperial culture. Singing our own music, in our dance along the unfolding of our destinies is what sets us free to be ourselves and to take responsibility for our part within the universal pattern unfolding. When they tried to make Jazz a classical tradition, Miles stopped playing! For making music into an imperial project destroys its ability to speak spontaneously a socially harmonious music.

Melancholics have to be very careful of this, for their capacity to unravel their deep realities depends upon them having a language with which to do so. They have to stick to things long enough for the patterns to reveal themselves and to develop the language to be able to articulate them. This is general across the species. They take time and rarely arrive swiftly at their insights and if they do, they spend ages being able to articulate them. Their creative process is often in steps and as a result they solve the puzzles as they go on in logical steps. In this they match an aspect of the creative process, for when an era begins the unfolding of its internal logic makes it predictable, but then there are those points at which there are shocking changes of direction, seeming to completely subvert the order, which utterly unseat the direction, and from which when the era resettles into its rhythm it will never ever be the same. This often shocks Melancholics who are lent to seeing the logical steps of order and who have trouble embracing Order's twin Chaos. This gives an insight into Melancholics for they are intimate with Order and find Chaos unsettling, whilst Sanguines love the arrival of Chaos, for it indicates new horizons, the Melancholic intimacy with Order, skews their vision in favour of seeing order and regularity of pattern, and habituate them to solving problems by bridging the gaps in Order. Consequently when Chaos leaves they return to trying to bridge the gaps so that everything returns to a normal order. This is how they are wired, but they must remember that because they are naturally fixated upon this aspect of the Creation, this does not mean that it is the entire picture, and developing the capacity to see through the eyes of Chaos is also a part of what perfects them. It begins to pull their envisioning into a clearer more precise manner of understanding existence.

And here we enter into another aspect of the archetypes, because in Know Yourself Choleric's chapter on The Mixes we looked at the creational realities of The Pen - The Qalam - and The Lawh - The Tablet. The Qalam writes upon The Lawh, what is, was and will be. We said that the Feminine Archetype was The Lawh and the Masculine Archetype The Qalam. We looked at how the Feminine Archetype expresses the potentialities of The Cold and The Wet, and how the Masculine Archetype expresses the potentialities of The Hot and The Dry. The Melancholic combines The Cold and The Dry holding in tension these two Archetypes within its patterned form. Shaped by the dance of love between these two potentialities, expressing the love and the desire to be known and to sing the realities hidden within the Unity. The Melancholic knows that, "The ink is dry and the pen is lifted.", whilst The Sanguine knows that the sincere prayer and passionate desire changes the pattern of the decree.

The three bio-types within the Melancholic species:

- Melancholic-Phlegmatic
- Melancholic-Sanguine
- And Melancholic- Choleric

Each express very different Melancholic possibilities. Appearances sometimes so different that you begin to wonder if they are actually Melancholics at all, until you pay close attention to their impulse natures. As a Melancholic you express the Feminine passive principle, which gives you very different possibilities for moving and manifesting things. You need the active energies often through interaction with others, the Melancholic-Phlegmatic more so than its other cousins, Melancholic-Sanguine and Melancholic-Choleric. You are inwardly directed and so you have a tendency to be more attached to the idea than the physical manifestation, and you tend to force the manifestation to fit the idea, even to the point of believing that the more it fits the idea the more beautiful it is. The Sanguine would tend to disagree with you! These are different ways of seeing and beginning to see through the eyes of Chaos enables you to develop a more complete view of the creative process.

The Melancholic Forest

The differences between Melancholic types understood by grasping how the servant aspect of the temperamental mix, affects the manner of expression of the Melancholic. The master is the Melancholic in their temperamental mix and its servants are expressed through the seat of the Melancholic. The Phlegmatic gives Phlegmatic tactics to the Melancholic, the Sanguine gives Sanguine tactics to the Melancholic and the Choleric gives Choleric tactics to the Melancholic. In the Know Yourself Method we only consider the base or master temperament and the second most dominant, since the others don't have as great an effect as the interaction of these two, and as you become more familiar with your own internal workings you will tend to work out how the other elements express themselves in you, as you confront different circumstances and various stages of health.

- Melancholic-Phlegmatic: The melancholic provides the base and the phlegmatic traits serve the melancholic impulses. This is a complementary mix, meaning that the behaviour of these types is consistent as the two types mix well.

- Melancholic-Sanguine: The melancholic provides the basis and the sanguine traits serve the melancholic impulses. This is one of the non-complementary mixes. This type is the most inconsistent of the non-complementary mixes, and can seem almost bipolar, making them particularly unpredictable.

- Melancholic-Choleric: The melancholic provides the basis and the choleric traits serve the melancholic impulses. This is a hot, volatile and focused   melancholic, with access to both hot and cold strategies.

Nature or Nurture

There is that ever present debate of Nature or Nurture. It doesn't go away and it never will. On the extreme wings of the Nurture debate comes the Tabula Rasa crowd, who believe that the newborn child is a blank slate that society must write upon to shape and make their plastic nature into the kind of human that the society desires. Education, which comes from the Latin educere means to lead out, and the Tabula Rasa crowd will always reduce education to a political and economic project. The Nature crowd at the extreme end sees the human being as a bundle of impulses and desires which should be left autonomously expressed and politically and socially uncontrolled. They see education as a project of freedom to choose. Timelessly, societies and civilisations will always be caught upon this spectrum, forging their place upon it. Nature and nurture both play an undeniable part in your development and the neglect of either can have disastrous consequences upon your capacity to fulfil your potential.

You come into the world with impulses, reflexes and patterns of orientation. In your early years you wrestle with your ability to express and manifest yourself within your social context. It is here that the shape of your psyche is determined by your social experiences, prompting the psychoanalyst Erik Erikson to coin the term 'psycho-social'. This affects how you develop your capacity to find your expressive way within your society. It affects how you connect, what you expect from connection, how safe you feel in the world, etc.

An education which does not take into account the differences inherent in people and their very different needs, squeezes everyone into a mould and often labels failure to fit into this process as a social or mental pathology. A badge that you are in danger of choosing to wear for the rest of your life! And a failure to establish an educational core which allows for

101

coherent psycho-social formation establishes a society which is fragmenting. A people must have a sense of who they are and the capacity to speak their differing natures into the collective conscious capacity of the civilisation to meet its everydayness and future. There will always be an essential tension in education.

For you now, in the world today, embracing your own self development, remember that whatsoever your educational process has lacked or given to you, from where you are today you must choose where you turn, and what you intentionally engage, in order to unfold your potential. You have a responsibility to Nurture your Nature, regardless of what happened to you or didn't happen. Doing this will present you with your personal and social demons, angelic rescue, betrayals, heroism, defeats, victories and the panoply of human dramas that makes up the dramatic landscape of being human.

The Melancholic Phlegmatic

Introduction

I'm a Melancholic, but don't pin me down, leave me my space and watch my quiet, observant, insightful, brilliance. I am like the waters at the foundations of the earth, I flow through deep underground caverns and hidden places, seeking and searching for meaning and intuitive understanding. The hidden underground worlds that you may never see are deeply familiar to me. If you are impressed by my insights know that what you have seen is less than the tip of the tip of the iceberg. I cannot be contained, for I dwell in the foundations of things, and only come up for social connection when I wish. The strategies of the Melancholic and the Phlegmatic are seamlessly combined in me.

The World According to the Melancholic-Phlegmatic

I need my space. Leave me alone. If you want to befriend me, then give me the space to decide if and when I want to let you be my friend.

I am flexible, quiet, thoughtful and withdrawn. Whilst you may think that I don't do much, there is a lot going on under the bonnet and if I choose to connect with you, then you will taste the depths to which I have dived. I cannot help myself, and I often don't think very much of it. Because I need to dive deep, I need space for it and to make sense of the considerable treasures I uncover. Despite my quiet unassuming exterior I must plunge into the difficult, inaccessible spaces beneath the earth, I am drawn to depth in general and so I am drawn to depth in people and companionship. I have a sense of humour, but I am not made for light, pointless conversation. If I am forced to it, then you will get a taste of my observations and my dark penetrating humour.

I am quite focused but with a deep capacity for intuitive and often artistic exploration. My rational and logical intellect falls into deep spaces of intuition, and I can stitch them together coherently, but I need time to fuse these fundamental opposites. This is also the source of my incredible flexibility, and so you will be surprised to find me surviving in many niches in which you would not expect to find either a Melancholic or a Phlegmatic.

I may shun physical activity but my mind is incredibly active. You may find that I understand you, but please honour my need for space because it is such a need that I cannot be held responsible for what happens when you repeatedly violate my domain. It will not end well!

The Melancholic-Phlegmatic According to the World

We just can't figure you out. You're hidden in the hidden and you play left-field when we play right-field and you play right-field when we play left. Everyone is going forward and you're spiraling in circles, and what is more incredible, is that no one even notices. You have secrets that the secrets themselves don't know about, and many of them you will never ever speak of, and others will never ever know of.

Well mannered would describe you, and often your insults seem like compliments and the receiver may feel honoured, not realising that they should be feeling offended. Your quiet, steady ways makes you dependable but you are much overlooked. There is nothing flowery and drawing attention, you seem to shun these things and you engage us with your mind, if you so choose, and the emphasis is on your choice. We've tried hard to get close to you, but in reality, this is done completely on your own terms. Your capacity to go completely unnoticed whilst quietly and intelligently observing the show, makes for really funny conversations with the few fortunate ones whom you take into your confidence. However, if we do not keep your secretive confidence, we find ourselves locked out with no possibility of return.

Your intellect is perhaps what surprises us most. You observe long patterns patiently, and dredge them up with your intuitive genius. When you make observations, they are the result of time spent paying close attention to them, analysing them and grasping where they come from (sometimes you're actually wrong, but your arguments are water-tight). You dig deep, you explore, you analyse, and you understand. You also pause, for your natural doubt is strong and so you check, double check and triple check, your own thinking. If you were a little less standoffish perhaps your insights would be triply rather than doubly accurate. But we get you, you can't handle people close up and messy in your zone.

As a love interest, you surround yourselves in mazes and moats and dead ends. Earning your romantic trust is perhaps the hardest thing we will ever attempt. You will be interested, but will choose to live it out in your imagination, and we will never be aware of your emotional interest. I suppose to you it is easier that way, but life is messy and it is in the messiness that we learn most!

In conversation we've learned that we have to give you lots of time and silence. Your replies are both super slow and ultra fast, so there are those times when we don't quite know how to deal with you. You also close your shutters down over trifles quickly and calmly. So when we get it wrong, it is not long before you shut us out.

In working relationships we have to give you time, as you work at your own pace. We will get depth, thoroughness and insight. If that isn't what we want then you're definitely the wrong person for the job because you are very consistent in that regard

The Melancholic-Phlegmatic Impulses

You are the abyss itself. You are a deep well, dwelling in possibilities and diving and swimming in its depths. Coming up to the light of day is necessary, but that is not what you most desire to do. "Let them look at the treasures unearthed and make use of them", you say to yourself, as you disappear back into the depths. Some may have to chase the hidden song, but you cannot escape it. You always hear its sonorous tones, and its rhythms are known to you, and what is abundant is often not valued by those who possess it aplenty. Your Melancholic nature looks down into the structure and your Phlegmatic looks towards the essence. The Melancholic employs rationality and logic, whilst the Phlegmatic employs observation and intuition. You don't impose your meaning on the song, but you are always decoding it. To do this you need room for clarity, and for the few who can follow your depth-sounding genius, to speak and share insights. You would rather remain unknown.

Summary

The Melancholic-Phlegmatic is a quietly and deeply active, intellectually penetrating, intuitive and observant type. Give them lots of space and freedom to explore, and don't saddle them with projects that don't employ their natural skills (you will make them very ill). They are wonderful to be around when they will have you around, and it is an incredibly grounding and revealing experience. You have to wait for them to trust you and invite you into their very exclusive circle, and if you even noticed it then kudos to you! This type hides in plain view, without having to make any special effort.

The Melancholic Sanguine

Introduction

You are one of a kind. Tremendous possibilities, so much choice, oh dear! You contain the ability to express all of the temperamental possibilities in a fairly stable manner. You join opposites, which are surprisingly similar, contrary to initial appearances. This offers you great possibilities and so I repeat, 'Oh dear!' For with great possibilities comes a great challenge, for the non-complementarity of opposing types with surprising similarities, makes it hard for them to mix well. Your type is a challenge. But the coolness of your Melancholic base may be of assistance, for this offers you at least some stability from which to embrace the development of your nature. Earth and Air do not mix except as dust whipped into the Air, and in your case we could say that the dust dominates. This offers you access to deep Melancholic thought and intermittent Sanguine periods. The payoffs can be huge, but you really have to put the work in. Because you are joining polar opposites this work will be some of the most difficult for all the types. Since these opposites do not mix well, you are constantly tested by tremendous changeability. Even you don't know on which side of the bed you will wake up on any given day. To those around you and often to your own self, you can seem bipolar, and the more imbalanced you are, the worse it gets. Today they meet the Melancholic and tomorrow the Sanguine, and 15 minutes later the Melancholic again. Accepting your changeability is essential to your self-development. It is just what it is. You will have to learn to find the appropriate response to your circumstances in spite of your changeability, but remember always that you live with the outcomes or consequences. I call this choosing your pain, in this case it means choosing the pain of really working through to an appropriate response, or the pain of the consequences of your just responding purely based upon spontaneous reflex. If you are courageous enough to look the consequences in the eye and own them, then you will find a surprising willingness to work through things by attempting to be appropriate. If you fall for the trap of not owning your contribution to the consequences (despite what others do) therein lies a difficult, rocky and troublesome path, which robs you of wisdom.

You are a Melancholic with the ability to employ Sanguine tactics, communication and social skills, but you do this to fulfil Melancholic objectives. You are a thinking, creative, with an emphasis on the thought, though you are able to dive into the fuzzy arguments, and jump into spaces of fuzzy exploration where other Melancholics cannot go. You can be running with a logical argument and suddenly jump off to meander into seemingly unrelated ground, and then bring it back into Melancholic focus with rational and logical arguments that are simply brilliant. You relate the seemingly unrelatable. You are the most arty and exploratory of the Melancholics and your courage gets you into sticky situations.

Your digestion is naturally weak, but it is strong for a Melancholic, and your sense of adventure gets you into digestive trouble. This provides a metaphor that perhaps will be very useful in your life.

If you see a Melancholic who consistently has strong Sanguine social skills, explorations and creativity, you are witnessing a Melancholic-Sanguine. And if you find them wholly unpredictable, then you've definitely found one. It does, however, take time to distinguish them from the Sanguine-Melancholic, their non-complementary sibling. Once you learn to distinguish between them I promise you that you will find ample entertainment.

The World According To The Melancholic-Sanguine

I'm a playful thinker. I turn ideas upside down and poke around endlessly. No, my reserve isn't a pretence, and yes, I am reserved and I can also be remarkably friendly, but I do need my space and can find it in the midst of crowds. People find this aspect of myself difficult, as they often can't quite decide whom they are dealing with. I get bored with people easily. I don't have the patience for fuzzy, badly thought out arguments and I filter everything through thought. I have this capacity to hold multiple, often contradictory, opinions. This further confuses others. You will find me setting goal oriented lists and planning my way through the world. I need a plan, which I can abandon but always for another plan. I can, however, deep dive into an area where I have the scent of something interesting, and I will often just keep diving until I find what I'm looking for. If I don't sharpen the discipline of my thinking skills I can end up finding what is not there.

Commitment to a project is very much dependent on both thinking and feeling. I have to give them both a place, as they are both strong, though unlike the Sanguine-Melancholic, in my case thought triumphs. Once I'm committed, the journey has to be pleasurable, but I need to spend time on my own, in order to maintain clarity. I need to work alone but I also need company, and I'm creative enough to find ways to square the circle.

I'm a Melancholic with well-developed social skills, but I am a Melancholic, so if the company is not prepared to explore ideas, I swiftly lose interest. I will use Sanguine stories and anecdotes to make points, and my jokes are intended to make a point, or to overturn the direction of the conversation, often forcing the conversation in completely different directions. I can see now that this may be exhausting and sometimes infuriating, but this is how I am. I swing from thought to feelings and back to thought again, but if you look carefully, you'll see that all of the conversation serves the development of the thought. I will often launch into extended explorations of matters and issues with the astounding attention to detail of a Melancholic. If you need to explore complex ideas and come up with creative well thought out solutions, then you want me on your side.

The Melancholic-Sanguine Traits According to the World

You can be a bit difficult to keep up with. You never stop thinking and exploring. You can be easy to speak to but something about you reminds us to stay on guard. That natural reserve never goes away even when we're close, and in the moment you can be as trusting as a Sanguine and then suddenly, as suspicious as a Melancholic. Your company is stimulating but as we get relaxed you change the script and change it again. You are compassionate, easygoing and generous but you also possess boundaries that we are not even aware of, and if we step over them your defensive mechanisms just swing into gear and you can be off swifter than a bird's flight. We thoroughly enjoy your conversations but there is always something in the background that tells us to be careful.

You open doors and are a great companion, but is it too much to expect you to stick around?

You are always off on another adventure, or project, or something, and once you're off, you're off. You don't have the optimism of a Sanguine though it seems so at first, but you certainly do have their exploratory trait and you could convince Caesar not to cross the Rubicon (but then he wouldn't be Caesar!), with incredibly creative and persuasive arguments, and then you're off to take residence where the next thing will happen. You don't stick around, and even when you do, wind and earth separate and like the wind and earth you evaporate and disappear, moving on from one interest to another.

And if you think that that was a complaint! You have no idea what dealing with you is like. You change direction convinced of your bearings by that mercurial intellect of yours, and if you bother to tell us, you've a watertight argument already prepared, decided and argued. You shoot us down after you've proceeded in another direction, leaving us lying on the ground that you led us to in the first place, and then we'd better be able to get up and keep up! At the same time, because you don't like having to deal with all the details, you expect us support you seamlessly. For this we would strangle you if you did not have the uncanny ability to spot what's coming next three steps in advance. This intellect gives you an arrogance that isn't so much a lack of humility, as it is a capacity to jump into the heat of situations with the confidence that you can handle it. More often than not, if you took the time to ask for advice we would have directed you to another less heated possibility in which success might be easier to achieve. Yes you've an incredible intellect, but talk to us, we have intellects and intuitions too!

Oh, and most infuriatingly, you sulk like a Melancholic and then avoid like a Sanguine, the worst of both worlds. So, when sulking you stick your head in the sand, ostrich like, and pretend that the problem will just go away. And if you can't find a place to stick your head in the sand, then you just zone out and go awol whilst in the midst of the crowd. How your mother did not strangle you in childhood remains a miracle! Oh, and yes, your sulking comes before your avoidance but they follow closely upon the heels of the other.

We can't contain you, but you contain yourself, and then when you realise that you've contained yourself, you rebel. You are both compelled to close your options down and to keep them open! Heaven help us!

It will never be perfect! Stop chasing after perfection! Stop waiting for the perfect time! And stop jumping off prematurely because you become anxious that what you envision might not happen.

Can you be surprised that we run away?

The Impulses of the Melancholic-Sanguine

Whist the Sanguine-Melancholic stands at the lip of the abyss, you will have plunged deeply into the it, in order to capture the volcano of possibilities, so that they can be made manifest in the world. You dive, gather, organise, think and draw potentialities together into coherence. This is what you were made for. Though you can be inspirational, you are more interested in transforming ideas, which have practical application. It is as if this deep creativity drives you to the need to see a practical manifestation not as a demonstration, but that it actually works. You are fixated upon combining thought and creativity so that it works but in the abyss, thought dominates. Whilst with your sibling the Sanguine-Melancholic, the creative impulse dominates that of thought. You solve the puzzles as puzzles and show a clear way forward.

Your challenge is to balance your Earthy Melancholic thought, which can tend towards strong ideological frameworks, with your creative impulse to make something manifest. If the thought framework becomes too fixed and inflexible then the wind cannot flow through. Remember that the map is not the terrain and you, as a mapmaker, will often mistake the map for the terrain. Only discipline, practice and humility will save you from this. Remember that others have thought too and that it differs from yours.

You have to know when to hand over, whilst you have an incredibly wide array of possibilities, there are some things which you simply will not be able to consistently muster the enthusiasm to continue doing over time. Some things have their people, who are enthused by just those things that don't enthuse you and if you learn to build alliances, you will reach the capacity for mastery.

In intimate relationships you are guarded, this is the Melancholic, though you can appear like a Sanguine in courtship, you just employed this possibility and in the security of your relationship you settle into your Melancholic need for safe, secure stability and space. Complete with Melancholic suspicions. Then you've this capacity for incredible generosity, which will frequently be abused, because often when we habituate people to receive from us they just get accustomed to receiving. The challenge of wisdom is to know when receiving becomes giving, when giving is actually withholding, and when withholding is enriching. The fiery crucible of relationships will teach you deeply and maintaining borders between your stuff and theirs is essential, if you want to be able to maintain the kind of relationship structure necessary for you to learn how to manage relationships wisely. Giving too much space for people to do as they wish with you will only result in your coming down hard, sharp and strong like a guillotine.

You need an artistic pursuit, if you are ever to grasp and master your natural rhythms. Here you have to step beyond your theoretical frameworks and encounter your raw energy as it is, and without some regular development of your intuitive and artistic facets you will find it too hard to gain the self connection necessary to work through this. You need routine and variation and finding the balance is an especially difficult one for you. Yes, with time you will learn to stop overextending yourself for overextension comes with this territory.

Summary

The Melancholic-Sanguine is one of the non-complementary forms that it is particularly difficult to master, for they are tested with an incredible array of possibilities. Basically, we have a pioneering, thinking creative who has an eye to stability. This is a thinking creative, who finds and creates innovative solutions. The contradictions and correspondences between the Melancholic and Sanguine traits is both the source of your strengths and of your challenges.

The Melancholic Choleric

Introduction

Melancholic-Cholerics are naturally quite focused like their other sibling the Choleric-Melancholic. These are lions of thought, energetic and intellectually confrontational. The earth is heated by the fire, so whilst stability is craved, change is also required. Here is a thoughtfully challenging intelligent form that is focused, and moves situations and thoughts along, in logical stable steps. The choleric leaps to solutions, but is constrained by the earth, the flashing leaps of insight have to be governed by a rational frame, in contrast to the Choleric-Melancholic in whom the Melancholic serves the Choleric. Here we may think of hot earthen bricks with the capacity to heat themselves up. When superheated they are like armour-piercing warheads, drilling into the core of what matters. When warm they bring warmth, comfort, and a stability that retains the capacity for change. Since both Earth and Fire are dry there is an incredible capacity to remain focused. This type is dominated by thought and if they are building projects they will be focused upon stability.

Here there is a deliberate attitude of inflexibility, but paradoxically, they will upend the intellectual edifice in order to ensure stability. There is less of a tendency to burn out, in contrast to the Choleric-Melancholic. However, when they do, they progressively become very melancholic and incredibly conservative as they compulsively seek stability. Their metabolism slows down and they literally become stuck, with conditions such as constipation, eruptive conditions and deep depression. Because this is an emotionally unstable type, fear, anxiety and deep depression, with flashes of extreme anger, are to be expected when they are unwell and imbalanced. They should guard the health of their livers, digestion and bowel health.

This emotionally not very stable form, needs to protect itself and especially their personal space. They maintain hard, sharp boundaries, and will tend not to engage if they don't want to. If you encroach beyond their boundaries and impose yourself, they will let you know that you are unwelcome. However, when relationships are established they protect, deploying their choleric traits in the process.

Their tendency to stability makes self-development easy for them, but they have to ensure that they guard stability, as they will become anxious and resort to psychodramas to ensure that their stability is restored. Stability and security are a must for this type. It must be understood that there is a narrow range of emotional stability and health, and so it is essential that this type maintains a good balance. Their digestion is weak, but it is also one of the strongest amongst Melancholics in general. They must maintain dietary discretion if they are to maintain their health. They should see this as an element of their necessary boundaries.

Like all Melancholics they are introverts, but this is an introvert with controlled bouts of extroversion. Yes, they can be incredibly social but this is in order to fulfil an objective and more often than not, the objective will be connected to knowledge.

This is a Melancholic with Choleric tactics. They are able to think things through and employ choleric tactics with a focus on the world of thought and theory. They are practical, yet idealistic, intellectually courageous but given to bouts of procrastination, and when procrastination increases, they need to do some soul searching and to take stock of their options and activities. Loss of access to their Choleric tactics and tendencies is a certain forewarning of illness and imbalance. However, if you see choleric strategies employing melancholic tactics, then know that you are dealing with a Choleric-Melancholic.

The World According to the Melancholic-Choleric

I need my space and I need to work things out. Getting in the way of that isn't a good idea, and you will not like my reactions. If I am nice about it, don't mistake that for weakness, for if you persist, then you deserve what you get. I find too much company exhausting and I don't trust easily, so if you wish to befriend me, then you'd better be prepared to take your time. Respect my personal zone and remember that I don't forgive easily.

I am goal oriented and need rational logical layouts to my projects. They have to make sense from the beginning. Practicality will always dominate but I do have a tendency towards idealism, and this will often slow my projects down. I will tend to discuss my projects and will look for confirmation but I can be a bit prickly about criticism. However, if criticism is articulated in terms that make sense, I will tend to consider it. I don't have a lot of patience for criticisms which are not rationally and logically presented.

I can alternate between times of self-doubt procrastination and clear, direct action. I have to really work things through before I start them. Once I start I proceed on my terms, and so the time to get me to reflect on what I do is during the phase of reflection, thinking and planning. I don't do things that don't make sense so when I decide on a course of action I have really thought it through. I don't need to win as much as I need what I'm doing to be stable, but I do like winning and don't be surprised at my capacity for subterfuge, and strategy, but in my own estimation I am fairly straightforward. I expect people to be straightforward with me and will punish those who are not. Don't always expect a fair hearing if you get on the wrong side of me and especially not if I view what you've done as a betrayal.

I can employ fairly good and effective people skills if you respect my boundaries and avoid challenging my preference for stability. I am interested in the strength and veracity of ideas and your ego comes second to this.

The traits of the Melancholic-Choleric According to the World

You are courageous thinkers, and defend the status quo whilst at the same time challenging it. Your idealism and love of the world of thought astounds us and we just wish that you, perhaps, could love people just as much. We love your focus and fear your sharp tongue. This really comes to the fore when you are defending an argument that you've had the time to think about. Your dry, penetrating wit can surprise us whilst in some of your species humour seems altogether lacking. Please preserve some feeling for our feelings. Please!

You don't accept us as friends unless you wish to and we'd best really take our time, but you can be so prickly at times that you just chase us away. You just don't let us in easily and when we do get in behind your firewall, your idealism can make it a difficult zone to survive in, and man do you hold a grudge.! Our apologies don't ever seem to be enough. We need thick skins to survive proximity, but you will fiercely defend us once we're in. And seeing you make quick work of anyone who attacks us, makes us glad that we have you on our side.

Your suspicion is difficult to deal with and you really need to practice making excuses for others. And we understand that you are also severe and suspicious with yourself. So though we may know that you didn't just single us out exclusively for your suspicion, the sharpness with which you deliver your reprimands makes it difficult to bear.

A little more flexibility would help and make life around you somewhat easier, but perhaps this is too much to ask.

Opposing you is tough, you have an arsenal of arguments and you have to win and you get upset so easily. We have to really choose our arguments with you because they will invariably end up as fights and we need the skills of a diplomat.

When supporting you we often end with wounds as we step on triggers that we didn't even know were there. Yes we love you, but it can be difficult.

The Melancholic-Choleric Impulses

You focus on the form of things and you quickly shut your options down to get to decisions. You are goal oriented and solve your problems methodically, with focused rational and logical arguments. You have a need to be steady but brisk and you need to lay down clear pathways and boundaries as you work your way through things.

Often your love of the idea causes you to miss what is in front of you especially when you are pushing towards a conclusion. This is the cost of your impulse and so you must be careful towards the conclusion of things. The dry energies predominate in you and this does not afford you a lot of flexibility, especially with regard to your health. Accepting this really makes you more effective. This dry energy doesn't allow you tremendous emotional flexibility and so you have to be conservative and careful in this regard. You hurt easily and take a long time to recover. However you have a tendency to be able to function whilst hurt. Please don't abuse this.

A large social circle is likely to be exhausting for you and perhaps you should prioritise the quality of your friendships over the quantity. In other words, the depth of connection comes before the breadth of the circle of friends.

Returning to your weakness for idealism, if you are not healthy and rested you will find that this will dominate. It can function as a red flag, which indicates the state of your physical and psychological health. The more you can hold yourself to the capacity to look and look again in order to see past your ideas, the healthier you often are. When this capacity is lacking you may want to consider going to bed earlier for a few consecutive days and if this doesn't help then you need to take more comprehensive action.

Summary

The Melancholic-Choleric is a complementary mixture, with incredible possibilities that come at a price. The form is relatively easy to master. You require intellectual challenge and depth, even if it is seen as manual activity. Solving puzzles and pulling disparate ideas together into a coherent whole is something you excel at. Your creativity is one that solves problems like puzzles.

You are idealistically fair and protective. You don't like large circles of friends and should not fight against your tendency to keep your circle small, but of deep connection. You need stability and that is necessarily a narrow band within which you can healthily maintain it.

Putting It All Together

Introduction

We have examined the Melancholic and their three possible expressions. Their famous capacity for thought, analysis and doubt is something we are all familiar with. This is just how they're wired. I hope that you learnt lots, had fun and noticed some new things. The point is to develop an intuitive grasp of the Melancholic and learn how to deal with them, and of course, since this is a book written for Melancholics, you should have become a little clearer and more comfortable with yourself. You should now be ready to use this information to be a better Melancholic or to just deal with Melancholics (Yes they will pour cold water on your best ideas! Be prepared and make use of this). We are now at the fourth book, and so we're past the middle of the series and on our way down the homestretch. And yes! I have taken a long time to finish this series! Have you guessed what my type is yet? Please continue the journey with the coming books and just repeatedly dip into these treasures, they were designed to be dipped into as a reminder and reflection on our difficulties dealing with people. Be gently honest with yourself (Melancholics you already question and triple question yourself, so please be true but gentle). Compassion towards ourselves can sometimes be the space in which we learn to be compassionate with others. Recognise your antics and have a giggle please, look at your impulses and motivations, from a place that frees you to address them, to naturally bring the best out of yourself. Time, success, failure, persistence and practice are your greatest friends on the journey. Let's re-examine the lessons we have learned, but remember that there is a lot more detail in the book.

The Lessons

The lessons are very simple:

1.   Work with yourself not against yourself. You are you. You possess the fundamental qualities and impulses that you do. You would do well to get to know them very,

very well. That is the whole point, 'Know Yourself'. Different situations will invariably surprise you as your possibilities reveal themselves.

2. Learn about your default reactions and what triggers them. Understand how that happens, ignore the why initially and really focus upon the how. Learn when they are useful and when they are not. Then work at becoming more appropriate and this will bring wisdom.

3. By now you should realise that the other types have their natural strengths. Make life easy for yourself and copy them when you see that they have a natural genius for certain types of situation. Your arsenal of responses will increase.

4. Pay attention, reflect and change. Then pay attention, reflect and change. Then pay attention, reflect and change. Do it again. And again. Ok, by now I think you get the point!

By paying attention we begin to grasp the nature of the warp and weft of the tapestry of existence, and we become better at understanding potentialities, possibilities and outcomes. Of course, we will get it wrong but celebrate getting it wrong and really reflect on what happened and how you misread the situation. Often we learn more from our errors than we do from our correctness.

Remember that people are what they are. They can change themselves and you can change yourself. Address that which you have the power to change, Yourself! Just be forgiving of the errors of others and ensure that you don't get caught by the faults which you have observed. That is hard work!

Benefit from the perspectives of the other types and practise empathising with their perspectives. You don't have to accept it and it may be quite crazy, but rather, try to understand where those perspectives come from and how their experiences have contributed to their peculiar worldview. Invariably, this habit leads you to really examine your own perspectives. Differences in the creation are a mercy!

Now in the words of Michael Jackson,

I'm starting with the man in the mirror

I'm asking him to change his ways

And no message could have been any clearer

If you want to make the world a better place

Take a look at yourself and then make a change

You are part of existence, therefore when you have changed, all of existence has changed.

Putting It Into Practice

Pay attention, reflect and change! Change, pay attention, reflect and continue. Let's wake up to the vast subtle tapestry of ourselves and the entire universe. As you change, what you see changes, and as what you see changes, your options usually expand. You become freer to act according to wisdom. Keep studying how changing our behaviour transforms our perspectives, until you are convinced of your capacity and achieve victory in embracing this aspect of your possibilities. Study the jewel that is appropriateness, for wisdom lies within it and keep going until you see how that necessarily varies from creature to creature, and type to type.

The Dramatic Structure of Living

Melancholic! Life is a drama and contrary to your worries and anxieties, if you act by wisdom it ends well. Check out the seven patterns of stories Melancholic. You'll enjoy that one.

Listen to the stories of others. Hear their orientations. Marvel at their optimism and pessimism. You have much to learn from your opposite biotype, the Sanguines. And if you are married to a Sanguine, then forgive me for giggling!

Enjoying & Employing Natural Strengths

Enjoy your natural strengths and employ them. Observe the natural strengths of others and study how to benefit from them. Now, that is pretty simple in principle, but by now we all know how difficult that will be to put into practice.

Don't Be Phased by Weaknesses

Enjoy your natural strengths and employ them, and don't be phased by your weaknesses. Weaknesses are the price of strengths. Observe the natural strengths and weaknesses of others and study how to gain from them. That will really help you to appreciate your own strengths and weaknesses. Now, that is pretty simple in principle, but by now we all know how incredibly difficult that will be to put into practice.

The Next Step

If you want to learn more about the other types read:

- Know Yourself Sanguine - This explores the Sanguine and the different sanguine mixtures;

- Know Yourself Phlegmatic - This explores the Phlegmatic and the different phlegmatic mixtures;

- Know Yourself Choleric - This explores the Choleric and the different Choleric mixtures;

Ok, now I am off to start writing Know Yourself Phlegmatic. Heaven help me!

www.ingramcontent.com/pod-product-compliance
Lightning Source LLC
Chambersburg PA
CBHW050127280326
41933CB00010B/1281